Socialist Workers Party

THE REVOLUTIONARY
ROAD TO SOCIALISM

ALEX CALLINICOS

Second edition February 1986

First published September 1983
Published by the **Socialist Workers Party**,
PO Box 82, London E3.

ISBN 0 905998 53 7

Printed by A. Wheaton & Co., Ltd., Exeter
Typesetting by Kate Macpherson.
Design by Roger Huddle [Artworkers].

The Socialist Workers Party is one of a group of socialist organisations linked
internationally:

AUSTRALIA: **International Socialists**, GPO Box 1473N, Melbourne 3001.
BRITAIN: **Socialist Workers Party**, PO Box 82, London E3.
CANADA: **International Socialists**, PO Box 339, Station E, Toronto, Ontario.
DENMARK: **Internationale Socialister**, Morten Borupsgade 18, kld, 8000
　　Arhus C.
FRANCE: **Socialisme International** (correspondence to Yves Coleman, BP 407,
　　Paris Cedex 05).
IRELAND: **Socialist Workers Movement**, PO Box 1648, Dublin 8.
NORWAY: **Internasjonale Sosialister**, Postboks 2510 Majorstua, 0302 Oslo 3.
UNITED STATES: **International Socialist Organization**, PO Box 16085,
　　Chicago, Illinois 60616.
WEST GERMANY: **Sozialistische Arbeiter Gruppe**, Wolfgangstrasse 81,
　　D–6000 Frankfurt 1.

CONTENTS

Alex Callinicos is a leading member of the Socialist Workers Party. His previous publications include *The Revolutionary Ideas of Karl Marx*, published by Bookmarks in March 1983, and (with Mike Simons) *The Great Strike*.

INTRODUCTION

THE CASE FOR SOCIALISM is overwhelming. All around us are the signs of a world in crisis.

Most obvious is the world economic slump, which means in Britain and other advanced countries mass unemployment on a scale undreamt of since the 1930s. Despite all the protests of our Tory rulers, no serious commentator expects unemployment in Britain to fall much below its present level of over four million.

The slump spells catastrophe for the poor countries of the Third World. There are 800 million people hovering on the brink of starvation in Africa, Asia and Latin America. For many of them international recession means the difference between survival and death. This is evident in the north-east of Africa, in countries such as Ethiopia and Sudan where ten million people are threatened with death by starvation, and where hundreds of thousands have already perished.

In the 1930s economic depression bred war and dictatorship. The same is true of the world today. The rulers of most states can hold on to power only by the open use of force. In such Central American countries as El Salvador and Guatemala right-wing regimes have turned massacre into a routine method of government.

More dangerous still are the rivalries between states. Resources that should be used to feed the hungry are squandered on ever more costly and destructive weapons. Half a million pounds is spent on 'defence' every minute of every day.

The inevitable consequence is war. The slaughter goes on throughout the globe — in the terrible war of attrition along the Iran-Iraq border, in the shanty-towns of Beirut, in the wastes of Afghanistan. Usually at least one super-power is involved: thus the Reagan administration has armed and backs the right-wing *contras*, the guerillas fighting to overthrow the revolutionary regime in Nicaragua.

Of course, the greatest threat comes from the arms race between the two super-powers themselves. After a brief thaw in the 1960s and 1970s, the Cold War has burst out again with redoubled vigour. Both sides have introduced new nuclear weapons in Europe, and invest in 'first-strike' missiles which make a mockery of the claim that this armoury is not there to be used, but to deter. And now Washington's Star Wars programme of space weapons, and its Russian counterpart, threaten to give the arms race yet another, even more dangerous twist.

The most probable outcome of slump and rearmament is, as in the 1930s, world war. But a Third World War would truly be a war to end all wars, destroying the earth in a nuclear holocaust.

Underlying all these different manifestations of crisis — unemployment, starvation, and war — is the economic social system which now embraces the entire globe, capitalism. Based on the competitive pursuit of profit and the exploitation of wage-labour, capitalism is the cause of all the disasters which afflict humanity today. Its remorseless logic means that people starve while food is stockpiled, coal mines are closed down while old-age pensioners die of hypothermia every winter, new missiles are built while hospitals are shut.

These bizarre priorities do not go without challenge. Around the globe, struggles have burst out which resist the logic of capital. In Britain in 1984 and 1985 the miners waged an epic struggle. For twelve months the women and men of the mining communities stood up to all the might of the British state, and were only defeated because they were shamefully deserted by the leaders of the trade union movement. Yet even in their defeat the miners were an inspiration to socialists throughout the world.

1984 and 1985 also saw an explosive wave of struggles in South Africa, where black people took to the streets to challenge the obscene racism of the apartheid regime. Braving the guns and whips of President P W Botha's brutish security forces, the black masses of South Africa created the worst crisis for white power in its entire history, one in which for the first time the African working class, increasingly organised into unions, began to play a central role.

These struggles, and others like them, raise the question: what is the alternative to the present system? The answer, at one level, is evident — socialism. A socialist society, in which the people of the world collectively control its resources, offers the only solution to capitalism's multiple disasters.

But what sort of socialism? During the last great crisis, that of the 1930s, working people looked to socialism as the way out of a world of poverty, unemployment, and violence. Two main traditions embodied these hopes. The Communist Parties claimed to stand for the victorious socialist revolution which occurred in Russia in 1917. The Labour Party and similar social-democratic parties in other countries sought to achieve socialism by winning a majority of seats in parliament.

The record of both these traditions in the past 60 years has been one of defeat, disillusionment, and betrayal. What exists in the eastern bloc is Stalinism, a hideous parody of socialism. A monstrous despotism rules in the name of the working class but — as the experience of Solidarity in Poland showed — denies workers the most fundamental of all rights, the right to organise.

Equally, the Labour Party has not fulfilled the hopes placed in it. The three most important Labour governments, those of 1945, 1964 and 1974, administered the present system rather than seeking to transform society along socialist lines. Many loyal Labour supporters found it difficult to distinguish the policies of these governments from those of their Tory rivals.

For a brief period after Labour's defeat in the 1979 general election it seemed as if all this might change, as if the Labour Party might move sharply to the left, and become a fighting socialist movement. Constitutional changes believed to be favourable to the left were passed by Labour Party conferences and Tony Benn came within an inch of becoming deputy leader of the party in October 1981.

This shift to the left was short-lived. The old conservative alliance of parliamentary and trade union leaders re-asserted their control of the party. After the disastrous general election of June 1983, when less than two in five trade unionists voted Labour, Neil Kinnock was elected leader with a mandate to restore the party's electoral fortunes.

Under Kinnock the shift back to the right has accelerated dramatically. He refused to support the miners in their year-long struggle against the Tories, and denounced left-wing Labour councils who defied the law in order to defend local jobs and services. In the wake of the miners' defeat a witch-hunt was launched against socialists inside the Labour Party, especially supporters of the Militant Tendency. Many former left-wingers, most notably Ken Livingstone, swung themselves behind Kinnock's rightward drive.

The result is to ensure that any future Labour government will, like its predecessors, confine itself to implementing pro-capitalist policies, attacking the jobs and living standards of its own working-class supporters. The struggle for socialism can only be waged by breaking with Labourism.

Such a socialist alternative to Labour needs to base itself on the revolutionary Marxist tradition, which stands apart from the failures of social democracy and Stalinism. Both these traditions see the existing state as the main instrument of change. Theirs is a 'socialism' handed down from above. Revolutionary socialism, the third socialist tradition, is *socialism from below*, and looks to the power of the working class to transform society.

This is the socialist tradition founded by Karl Marx and Friedrich Engels, and continued most notably by Vladimir Lenin and Leon Trotsky. It is the tradition in which the Socialist Workers Party in Britain and its sister organisations in other countries stand.

For most of its existence, revolutionary socialism has been confined to small minority groups in the working-class movement. But at times of great crisis and upheaval, when the mass of workers are thrown into conflict with the state, revolutionary socialists have won mass support. We live today in such times. After the disastrous failures of Labourism and Stalinism, those socialists who seek a way out of a world of poverty, unemployment, and nuclear destruction must look to revolutionary socialism.

WHY CAPITALISM IS IN CRISIS

THE ORIGINS OF THE SLUMP

Probably the most common explanation of the world economic crisis is that it arises from factors outside human control. According to this theory the world is running out of natural resources. There just isn't enough to go round, they say, to keep the present population of the world alive at the standard of living (some of us) have come to expect.

This sort of explanation sees the years 1973 and 1974, when the price of oil rose fourfold, as the crunch point, a sign that the world had reached the limits of economic growth. We have no choice, its supporters suggest, but to accept lower living standards. As for the Third World, the problem is that people are breeding too much. Population is growing much faster than food production, and so it is inevitable that people will starve.

Theories of this kind are sometimes known as Malthusian, after the Anglican clergyman who was the first to argue that the source of poverty was that working people were having too many children. But the Malthusians are wrong. The growth in world food production has consistently kept ahead of the growth in population since the Second World War. The United Nations Food and Agricultural Organisation estimates that the average person needs 2,354 calories a day, and that the world produces about 2,420 per head — and could easily produce more.

The reason why 800 million people don't have enough to eat is that the most important producers of food are a handful of rich countries — the United States, Canada, Australia, Argentina. The farmers of these countries do not produce meat and grain out of love for their neighbours, but in order to make a profit. The trouble for those 800 million people in the Third World is that they don't have enough (or any) money to buy the food that the rich offer them. So they go hungry.

The situation is even more obscene than that. The profits of the rich farmers depend on the prices they can get for their products. The prices of goods fluctuate with changes in their supply and demand. When goods are scarce, their prices are high; when they are plentiful, their prices are low. Western governments actually create artificial scarcity in order to keep the prices of their farmers' goods high. The European Common Market's wine lakes and butter mountains are famous. In 1982, when there was a bumper harvest of champagne grapes, first-class champagne was turned into vinegar to keep the price — and profits — high. Expensive champagne hits only the rich; expensive butter, meat and grain hits the poor.

Now, in the United States, the biggest food producer of all, the government is *paying* farmers to keep a portion of their land out of production. So enthusiastic was the response to this government scheme that by March 1983 farmers had agreed to take 82.3 million acres out of production: 35 per cent of wheat acreage, 39 per cent of maize and sorghum, 43 per cent of rice. Grain prices rise as a result, and people who cannot afford to pay go hungry.

The operations of capitalism world-wide also wreck the agricultural systems of the poor countries. The starvation in north-east Africa reflects the way in which peasant farmers have been pushed into producing cash-crops such as coffee and cotton rather than the food their families need. Cash-crops can be exported to earn foreign exchange, which is desperately needed to pay off Africa's debt to the Western banks. This debt represents a higher share of the continent's income than that of Latin America. Famine in Africa mirrors the profits of Wall Street and the City of London.

Crises today are not caused by natural scarcity. In the past, when people starved, it was a result of harvest failure — there wasn't enough to go round. Now such scarcity is artificially created. Now we have *over*production. Not too little, but *too much* is produced — 'too much' not compared to people's needs, but to the profits of those who control the world economy.

The other popular explanation of the crisis claims that it is caused by workers being paid too much. You hear this in a variety of different forms. People say that the trade unions are too powerful, that they are holding the country to ransom. The Tory government and its supporters in Fleet Street say that workers are 'over priced' — in other words, their wages are too high.

The implication of this analysis (like that of the other) is that the way out of the crisis is to cut living standards. In this way, workers will 'price themselves into jobs': once wages have been cut far enough, then employers will find it worth their while to take on more workers, and unemployment can be cut.

Once again, this theory doesn't fit the facts. For one thing, what we are now confronted with is a *world* recession. In some countries there have been strong and militant trade unions and workers have been able to squeeze large concessions from the employers. Britain and Italy are the best examples in western Europe. But countries such as the United States and West Germany, where the unions are much less militant, have also been hit by the slump, in some cases very hard. So the strength of workers can't be the cause of international crisis.

It can't even explain what has happened in Britain. The Tory government points out that real earnings rose by 5.5 per cent between 1981 and 1984. This, they claim, is the reason why unemployment remains so high. This increase is, however, an *average* figure: it conceals enormous differences between high-paid and low-paid workers. The government's own figures show that the real take-home pay of a single man in the lowest-paid 10 per cent of the workforce rose by only 1.8 per cent in the six years after April 1978, while a single man in the highest-paid 10 per cent was 18.4 per cent better off at the end of this period!

The big business paper the **Financial Times** commented on 31 May 1985:

> The government has frequently given real wage increases as one of the causes for high unemployment, and argued that lower pay was needed

to price people back into jobs. However, the figures show that real take-home pay of the poorest single workers fell by nearly six per cent in the three years to April 1982, the period during which unemployment was increasing most rapidly.

Lower wages were accompanied by *higher* unemployment. So much for workers being 'priced into jobs'!

The idea that lower wages will solve the crisis isn't just wrong, it's mad. If workers' wages are lower, they can afford to buy fewer goods. Some of those now producing these goods will be laid off. *They* will have less money to spend, so demand will fall even lower, more workers will be laid off . . . and so on, in a vicious spiral.

The theory that high wages are the cause of the slump has one merit. Although mistaken, it unintentionally reveals the real source of the problem. Wages are too high compared to what? Certainly not people's needs. In order to live decent and fulfilled lives most working people would need much higher wages than they receive at present. Relative to what, then, are wages too high? The answer is, relative to *profits*. Wages are too high for employers to make what they regard as an adequate profit.

As in the case of the theory that scarcity is the cause of the slump, we come back to profits. Fields go unsown because their crops would not realise a satisfactory profit. Workers are unemployed because it isn't profitable to give them a job. The central conflict, then, is between the livelihoods of most people on this planet and the profits of the few. So to understand what is wrong we need to grasp what role profits play in the world economic system.

Capitalism – a class society

The basic insight into how societies like our own are run was provided by Karl Marx, who died a hundred years ago, in 1883. In his masterpiece, **Capital**, Marx pointed out that the economic system in which we live, capitalism, is a class society. The wealth produced in this system depends on the labour of those who work in the factories, mines and offices. As every strike shows, when this labour is withdrawn, capitalism is paralysed. Yet these workers do not control the economic system.

On the contrary, a tiny minority controls what Marx called the 'means of production' — land, factories, mines, and the machinery that is used to produce goods. One sociologist estimates that 1,000

companies dominate the British economy. Those who control
these companies, and their families, amount to between 25,000 and
50,000 people, less than 0.1 per cent of the population. It is this
tiny minority who control and dominate our lives.

The rest of us outside the charmed circle of the rich do not own
anything which gives us economic power. At best we may own our
homes — and that is a dubious benefit, making us the debtor of
some bank or building society. To earn anything more than the
pittance which those on the dole receive, we must sell our labour-
power, our ability to work, to the capitalist controllers of the
economy.

Why do these capitalists employ us? Out of the goodness of
their hearts? No — because it is on us that they depend for their
wealth. Production in the capitalist system does not take place to
meet people's needs. Its aim is *profit*. Goods are produced to be sold
on the market. They realise a profit when their price is higher than
it cost to produce them.

The crucial element in production is labour. Without it, production grinds to a halt. And workers have, from the capitalists'
point of view, the peculiar virtue that they can produce more than
it cost to employ them. A worker may, for example, take four hours
to produce the equivalent of his or her daily wages. But if he or she
works for another four hours every day, what is produced during
this time is pure profit for the capitalist.

It is this 'surplus-value', as Marx called it, what the worker
produces for the capitalist after replacing his or her wages, that is
the source of profits. The wealth of the capitalists derives from the
exploitation of workers — from the way in which workers are compelled to work for the capitalists, not only to replace their wages,
but to create profits.

This is what Marx described as the secret of capitalist production. It is usually assumed that capitalists and workers share the
same interests, that they are in the same boat, that there is some
'national interest' uniting them. This is not true. At the heart of the
capitalist system is the basic conflict of interest between capital and
labour which arises from the exploitation of the worker.

This doesn't mean, however, that all workers are reduced to
poverty. The situation is compatible with rises in workers' living
standards. Real wages have increased quite considerably in Britain
over the past century. But this increase has been accompanied by

an enormous rise in the productivity of labour — in the amount of goods each worker produces. So even if a worker is paid much more than he or she would have been a hundred years ago, he or she also produces much more. So the profits of capital have also risen. In *relative* terms workers are just as badly off, even if our standard of living has risen.

Profits and Crises

Capitalism, then, is an economic system based on production for profit. But it's important to understand why capitalists are so interested in profits, and what they do with them. It isn't a matter of capitalists being greedy — of their wanting profits to spend on wine, women and song (although often they are and they do). When the system is working well, at any rate, profits aren't blown by capitalists on high living; the bulk is reinvested in further production.

This is what Marx called 'the accumulation of capital'. Profits are squeezed out of workers in order to be themselves invested in squeezing out *more* profits, which are in turn reinvested . . . It is production for production's sake.

Why does this happen? Above all, because of the pressures of the system. Capitalism, Marx pointed out, is a *competitive* system. No single capitalist dominates the economy. Instead, a number of different capitalists compete with one another for markets. It is their economic rivalries which force capitalists continually to accumulate, to reinvest profits.

The capitalist who has the lowest costs is likely to dominate the market. So each must invest in improved machinery which will increase the productivity of his workers, and thus give him an edge over his rivals. Any capitalist who fails to keep up will eventually be driven out of business.

The pressure of competition thus compels capitalists to accumulate. When Marx wrote, in the second half of the nineteenth century, the economy was divided into large numbers of small capitalists none of whom dominated their market. Today firms are more likely to be vast semi-monopolies operating on a multinational scale. But the competitive pressures are the same.

For example, Ford UK is apparently obsessed by the fact that productivity in Japanese car plants is six times that of its own workers. The need to match Japanese productivity, or lose markets, leads to the introduction of new technology, and to attempts to reduce costs and speed up production lines.

The effects of competition were, Marx argued, paradoxical. On the one hand, capitalism is an immensely dynamic economic system. Economic rivalries constantly force capitalists to improve productivity and increase output, leading to an enormous expansion in humanity's power over nature. On the other hand, competition is the source of economic crises.

How this happens is as follows. Competition leads capitalists to reinvest their profits in improving productivity as a way of cutting costs. Now what higher productivity tends to mean is that the amount of plant and equipment each worker sets in motion increases. Imagine the mass of machinery as a ball and chain attached to his or her leg. As time goes on, this ball and chain gets larger and larger. A hundred years ago, building a house involved no more tools than a spade and a trowel — today it needs excavators, cranes, concrete mixers.

From an abstract point of view, this is no bad thing. It means that less and less human labour is required to produce a growing quantity of goods — or houses. We can rely instead on a growing mass of machinery.

But this development causes severe problems for the capitalist. For it means that he has to lay out an ever larger amount of money on plant and equipment for every worker he employs. Yet it is the *worker* who is the source of the capitalist's profits — his or her labour produces that surplus above his or her wages. So the cost of investments rises faster than the profits squeezed out of the workforce. In other words, the return that the capitalist gets on his investment, the rate of profit, falls.

This process, which Marx called the tendency of the rate of profit to fall, is fundamental to how capitalism works. It isn't something that any individual capitalist plans for. On the contrary, any investments he makes are intended to reduce costs and so undercut his rivals. And as long as he is the only one to have made this investment his profits will rise. But once everyone else has followed him, as they must if they are to avoid bankruptcy, then his advantage is wiped out, and the rate of profit falls.

The tendency for the rate of profit to fall is thus an unintended consequence of competition between capitalists. It is the source of the crises which regularly afflict the capitalist system. For there comes a point where the rate of profit has fallen so low that a slump begins.

Firms try to compensate for the falling return on their investments by grabbing a larger share of their markets. Capitalists compete for the labour and raw materials they need to increase production. Demand runs ahead of supply, and prices rise, pushing up costs and eating into profits. This is what happened in the early 1970s, the last time that the world economy experienced a genuine boom. In 1972–3 Western industrial production shot up by an astonishing 10 per cent. But the competition among capitalists which fuelled the boom also forced prices through the ceiling. Between 1971 and 1974 raw-material prices more than doubled. The crunch came when the price of oil quadrupled, precipitating the first great slump since the 1930s.

The fundamental cause of economic depressions is the low rate of profit. The weaker capitalists, who find it difficult to keep their heads above water at the best of times, go into debt and are driven out of business altogether. The stronger ones survive by cutting production and sacking workers. Resources are unused. Some of these resources are human — workers are laid off, school-leavers go straight to the dole queue. Others are material — factories are closed, machinery rusts. Waste takes place on an enormous scale.

Bizarrely enough, this waste is very useful to the capitalist system. It permits an economic reorganisation that will restore the rate of profit to a satisfactory level. The pressure of unemployment forces workers to accept lower wages and worse working conditions. And the smaller, less efficient capitalists go bust. The survivors can buy up their plant and equipment cheap.

This goes on until the rate of profit has risen to a level which the capitalists consider to be 'adequate'. When this point is reached, they are prepared to invest. Workers are taken on, there is more money around so demand for goods rises, and the economy begins to pick up. This carries on until we have a boom and the whole cycle starts off again.

Why shouldn't this succession of booms and slumps go on for ever? The short answer is that capitalism changes over time. It *ages*. What this means is that, as a result of competition, the capitalists get bigger and bigger. The hundreds of small individual employers of 100 years ago are replaced by a vast multinational corporation. And often the corporation is owned by the state, like Renault or BP or British Leyland.

This means that bankruptcy becomes a much more serious business. In the nineteenth century an individual employer could go bankrupt without damaging the national economy. This is no longer so in the case of the 1,000 big companies which today dominate the British economy (and the same is true of all the advanced industrial countries). If a significant number of these companies went under, that would break the back of the national economy.

So governments, of whatever colour, pump money into lame-duck firms. Margaret Thatcher has subsidised British Leyland on a massive scale and Ronald Reagan has propped up Chrysler, even though this goes against all their economic principles. In 1984 the 'free market' Reagan administration actually went even further: when one of the biggest American banks, Continental Illinois, went bust, the Federal Reserve Board intervened to stop a financial panic and effectively nationalised the bank.

What this means is that economic crises no longer play their role of restoring the rate of profit. Inefficient firms, if they are big enough, aren't wiped out, but are kept going. The system is clogged up with inefficient capitalists.

This situation is reflected in the persistence of inflation. In the past, prices rose during booms, and fell in slumps. Now they rise all the time. Recessions don't get rid of inflation, but only slow down the rate at which prices increase. In 1985 there were some four million unemployed in Britain, but the rate of inflation was about 5 per cent, a very high level by historical standards.

What is more, the times are past when one country could solve its economic recession at the expense of its neighbour — through massive restrictions on trade, for example, or by fighting a small war in Africa to grab new markets. Today we live in one *world* economy. The motor car or radio set 'made in Britain' is in fact made up of parts manufactured everywhere in the world — micro-chips from Sri Lanka, gearboxes from Spain, seat covers from India, copper wiring from Chile.

Each part of that world economy depends on the whole — and when recession strikes, it strikes everywhere, bringing bread queues in Poland, starvation in Mexico, mass unemployment in Britain.

This means that any policy of import controls to protect national trade is doomed to fail. Those who advocate such controls do so because they believe that imports cause unemployment. In fact, there is little evidence for this. One study of West German manufacturing industry showed that for every one job lost thanks to competition from cheap imports there were *forty-eight* lost by rationalisation, employers deliberately cutting their own work-forces in the quest for higher productivity.

Import controls don't make sense in a world economy. Countries that apply them invite retaliation. In 1980 the British government tried to cut textile imports from Indonesia worth £10 million. The Indonesian government responded by cancelling contracts for imports from Britain of chemical plant, oil equipment, and other goods worth £150 million. So who gained?

Protectionism isn't just economic nonsense. It encourages workers to believe that unemployment is caused, not by the capitalists who exploit them, but by their fellow workers in other countries. Yet these workers are often exploited — and thrown out of work — by the same multinational companies. British workers end up supporting their own employers in opposition to German, say, or South Korean workers.

The politics of import controls is nationalist, pitting countries against one another. It carries within it the danger, not just of trade wars, but of real ones. During the Great Depression of the 1930s, protectionism spread like wildfire. World trade shrunk, and states built up their armaments in order to win by military means what they could not gain by economic competition. Economic crises breed war.

Each slump becomes harder for the capitalist system to solve.

This does not mean that slumps are permanent. The cycle of growth and recession will continue as long as capitalism does. Capitalism is an anarchic system, in which production is not under collective social control, but is left to the chances of competition. This means that economic balance can only be achieved by blundering from one extreme to another, from boom to slump.

The capitalist system is at an impasse. The rate of profit is still too low for a genuine economic revival. **The Economist**, the big-business magazine, estimates that real wages in Britain would have to be cut by 19 per cent in order to restore the rate of profit to the level it was at in the 1960s. That is a far greater cut than anything Thatcher has been able to achieve, and would require confrontation with the labour movement on a scale that capitalists do not yet seem willing to contemplate.

The crisis has roots deep within capitalism. It can be ended only by abolishing capitalism and replacing it with a planned socialist economy. Collective democratic control on a world scale would end the anarchy of a system that staggers from slump to boom and back to slump again. Socialism would harness the immense productive powers created by capitalism — but it would use those powers to meet people's needs, not for the pursuit of profit. The working people of the world would co-operate together, rather than being chained to warring nation-states.

Socialism is essential. The only question is how to achieve it.

THE REFORMIST TRADITION

CAN SOCIALISM COME THROUGH PARLIAMENT?

Throughout this century working people in Britain have placed their hopes in the Labour Party as the means through which they could improve their lot and achieve a socialist society. Similar parties have played the same role in other parts of the world.

The political strategy pursued by these parties is that of reformism, or social democracy. (The breakaway SDP is a johnnie-come-lately, representing the extreme right wing of this tradition.) The idea behind this strategy is a simple one. However much more powerful the capitalists are than workers, the latter have one weapon: the vote. When it comes to election time, Sir Arnold Weinstock of GEC has the same power as a school cleaning lady. Moreover, there are, as we have seen, very few capitalists. By banding together and using the vote, workers can win a majority of seats in parliament, and thus capture political power.

The attractions of this strategy are obvious. It's simple and it seems to threaten no messy or violent confrontation with the capitalist class. Why, then, after eighty-five years of following the reformist recipe, are we no closer to socialism than we were in 1900?

There are three main reasons why this is so. The first is to do with how power is organised within the capitalist state on a day-to-day basis. Parliament is supposedly 'sovereign' — that is, it is meant to have supreme power in the state. The reality is quite different.

In practice, the elected chamber of parliament, the House of Commons, has little effective control over what the government does. Parliament passes the legislation presented to it by the cabinet. And even ministers are hemmed in by their permanent civil servants. Richard Crossman, a Labour cabinet minister in the 1960s, described in his diaries how his officials worked to tie things up behind his back, and sought to present him with *faits accomplis*. The television programme **Yes Minister** graphically shows the process at work.

The result is that Labour governments, once in power, find themselves willy-nilly pushed into merely continuing existing policies rather than making a radical break with the past. A good illustration is defence policy.

The 1945 Labour government was dominated by ministers who had served in Churchill's wartime coalition, and who were used to working closely with the Americans. The Foreign Secretary, Ernest Bevin, was one of the main architects of NATO. Prime Minister Clement Attlee took the decision to build an atomic bomb without even consulting the cabinet. And Chancellor of the Exchequer Hugh Gaitskell introduced a budget in 1951 which massively boosted defence spending. The Tories could not have done better.

The pattern was the same in later governments. In the 1960s Harold Wilson and his Defence Secretary, Denis Healey, bought Polaris missile submarines from the US in defiance of official policy decided at Labour Party Conference. In the 1970s James Callaghan agreed secretly to modernise these weapon-systems, and took the first steps towards having Cruise missiles in Britain.

But even when Labour governments *do* attempt to introduce new policies, they are usually prevented from doing so by economic pressures. As we have seen, capitalism today is an international system. This is most obviously so at the level of production, with multinational companies organising on a global scale.

Finance is also organised internationally. The big banks lend money to firms and governments all over the world. Capital is lent and borrowed on the money markets, outside the control of any government. Multinational corporations dispose of vast funds which they use to play these markets. By switching money from one currency to another they can force governments to change policies.

This is precisely what happened to Harold Wilson's Labour government in October 1964. It had been elected after thirteen years of Tory rule on a platform of far from radical reforms designed to modernise the British economy. These policies were not, however, acceptable to the money men, who switched their funds out of Britain, causing a slump in the value of the pound.

Harold Wilson describes what happened:

> The Governor of the Bank of England became a frequent visitor. It was his duty . . . to represent to the Chancellor and the Prime Minister the things that were being said abroad or in the City; to indicate to the Government the issues on which, in the City's view, it was necessary to win confidence . . .
>
> That is why we had to listen night after night to demands that there should be immediate cuts in Government expenditure, and particularly in those parts of Government expenditure which related to the social services . . .
>
> Not for the first time, I said that we had now reached the situation where a newly elected Government with a mandate from the people were being told, not so much by the Governor of the Bank of England but by international speculators, that the policies on which we had fought the election could not be implemented . . . The Governor confirmed that this was, in fact, the case.

Wilson caved in, and implemented the cuts demanded. The same thing happened again when he returned to office in March 1974. Labour had defeated a reactionary Tory government on a programme which promised a number of 'basic Socialist goals', including 'a fundamental and irreversible shift in the balance of power and wealth in favour of working people and their families.' Within little more than a year these promises had been scrapped. Wage-controls were introduced, and Tony Benn was removed from the crucial post of Secretary for Industry. Denis Healey introduced cuts in public spending which laid the basis of Thatcher's monetarist policies. Workers' living standards fell more drastically than they had for a century.

Nor is this purely a British disease. In June 1981 Francois Mitterrand and the French Socialist Party swept to power, ending twenty-three years of right-wing rule. They proceeded to implement a programme — much more radical than anything Labour has ever tried — of large-scale nationalisation.

The result was an acute financial crisis. Money poured out of the country as French and foreign capitalists alike passed a vote of no confidence in the Socialist Party government. Big business effectively went on strike, refusing to invest. The franc slumped. Mitterrand was forced to negotiate a huge foreign loan to prevent financial collapse. The loan came from the big banks with strings attached: the government adopted a programme of austerity measures involving sackings, closures, and cuts in real wages and in welfare services.

The effect of Mitterrand's surrender to international capital was massive disillusionment among working-class voters. Many swung over to the parties of the parliamentary right. Some went even further, and backed Jean-Marie Le Pen's Nazi *Front National*, which won 10 per cent of the French vote in the 1984 Common Market elections. Reformism's failure encouraged many white workers to see their black brothers and sisters as their enemy.

One lesson of this experience is that socialism cannot be achieved by any individual country acting on its own. The capitalist system is an international one, and can be overthrown only on a world scale. Yet Labour, and other reformist parties, persist in pursuing nationalist policies.

Labour's economic programme amounts to giving a large financial boost to the British economy, and using import controls to prevent foreign firms from taking advantage of this. But Labour does not explain, despite the experience of Harold Wilson and 1964, how they will prevent this economic expansion from being strangled by a financial crisis engineered by the money men and the multinationals.

But what would stop a new-style Labour government, one that was aware of the pressures from the civil service and the multinationals, and was determined to combat them, from succeeding? Here we run into the third, and most fundamental obstacle across the parliamentary road to socialism.

Reformist politicians tend to assume that the state is neutral. In other words, they believe that it can be used in the interests of working people. They may denounce the more undemocratic features of the state — the House of Lords, say, or (if they are feeling very brave) the monarchy. But they argue that once these features have been removed, everything will be OK. Left-wing councillors demand that the police should be made 'accountable', but they accept that the police are 'neutral'.

This assumption is based on a fallacy. It ignores the truth, uncovered by Marx, that 'political power . . . is the organised power of one class for oppressing another.' The state is *not* neutral. The way in which it is organised reflects and seeks to defend the interests of big business.

'Society is based on the death of men', the American jurist Oliver Wendell Holmes Junior liked to say. The core of the state is its repressive apparatus, the bodies of highly trained, well-paid, armed men and women who make up the army and the police. Their job is to defend the existing order against any threats to it. Usually this means no more than the police harassing black teen-agers and smashing picket lines, as they did during the 1984–5 miners' strike. But in a period of social and political upheaval the army would be used to crush any serious challenge to the wealth and power of the capitalist class.

This would happen even if that challenge came from the legally elected government. Anyone who doubts this should remember what happened in Chile. In 1970 the socialist Salvador Allende was elected president on a platform which sought to transform society by peaceful, constitutional means. The result was a series of confrontations with the American multinationals, the middle classes, and even some workers. Finally, on 11 September 1973 the army seized power. Tens of thousands of socialist and trade-union militants were slaughtered, including Allende himself.

There are many parochial British socialists who would say that Britain is a very different place from Chile: we do things differently here, thanks to a centuries-old tradition of peaceful and legal change. They forget that in the seventeenth century an English parliament cut a king's head off, and that in the early nineteenth century the army was used to crush working-class revolts in north-ern England and Scotland.

Those who have illusions in the mild and peaceloving nature of our rulers should consider the Falklands War. A Tory govern-ment, with the grudging or enthusiastic support of the entire establishment, was prepared to squander a thousand lives and billions of pounds to recapture a useless lump of rock in the south

Atlantic. Can anyone doubt that the capitalist class they represent would be prepared to wade through blood rather than lose control of the economy?

A hundred years ago, in 1886, the greatest British revolutionary, William Morris, pointed out the basic error made by the reformists:

> There are undoubtedly many who are genuine democrats who have it in their heads that it is both possible and desirable to capture the constitutional Parliament and turn it into a real popular assembly, which, with the people behind it, might lead us peaceably and constitutionally into the great Revolution . . . Those who think we can deal with our present system in this piece-meal way very much underestimate the strength of the tremendous organisation under which we live, and which appoints to each of us his place, and if we do not chance to fit it, grinds us down till we do. Nothing but a tremendous force can deal with this force: it will not suffer itself to be dismembered, not to lose anything which really is its essence without putting forth all its force in resistance; rather than lose anything which it considers of importance, it will pull the roof of the world down upon its head.

Nothing that has happened since 1886 has done anything to take away any of the force of these words. Rather, they stand up as a brilliant prophecy of the failure of reformist socialism in the twentieth century.

Far from being neutral, above classes, the state is an instrument of class rule. It is the final guarantee of class power. Reformism starts out trying to use this state. It ends up serving its class interests.

At one level this means passing laws to defend capitalist class interests: the attacks on trade-union rights being carried through by the Tories began as proposals by the 1964–70 *Labour* government. But ultimately it means defending the state against the very workers the reformists claim to represent.

So, in 1918–19, the Social Democratic Party in Germany, elected by massive workers' votes, allied themselves with the Imperial General Staff of the army to prevent the workers taking power. Together they presided over the use of right-wing soldiers (the Freikorps, many of whom later joined Hitler's Nazis) to murder thousands of left-wing workers throughout Germany.

Likewise, when the 30-year fascist dictatorship in Portugal was overthrown in 1974, it was the Portuguese Socialist Party who allied themselves to the Catholic Church and right-wing army officers to defeat demands from workers and rank-and-file soldiers for a socialist republic.

Labour ministers in Britain have been loyal servants of the British state. Merlyn Rees and Roy Mason, successively Secretary of State for Northern Ireland in the last Labour government, denied political rights to republican prisoners, allowed the use of SAS assassination squads, and presided over the use of torture by the Royal Ulster Constabulary.

The Nature of the Labour Party

There are many socialists in the Labour Party who would agree with many, if not all of the arguments set out above. Nevertheless, they believe that things need not be the same in the future. The Labour Party can be won to genuine socialism, they say. After all, it is the party of the working class. Socialists should be inside the Labour Party trying to push it leftwards.

The trouble with this argument is that it ignores the nature of the Labour Party, and so flies in the face of eighty-five years of experience.Every attempt to win the Labour Party to fighting socialism has failed.

Throughout its history socialists have argued over whether or not the Labour Party can be transformed. This was one of the main issues at the Second Congress of the Communist International in August 1920, when the British socialist William MacLaine declared, in words that have often been echoed since, that 'the Labour Party is the political expression of the workers organised in the trade unions.'

Lenin was quick to challenge this claim:

It is erroneous . . . Of course, most of the Labour Party's members are working men. However, what determines whether or not a party is really a party of the workers does not depend solely on a membership of workers but also on the men who lead it and its political tactics. Only that determines whether we really have before us a political party of the proletariat. Regarded from this, the only correct point of view, the Labour Party is a thoroughly bourgeois party, because, although made up of workers, it is led by reactionaries, and the worst kind of reactionaries at that, who act quite in the spirit of the bourgeoisie. It is an organisation of the bourgeoisie which exists systematically to dupe the workers.

Lenin summed this up by calling Labour a 'bourgeois workers' party'. It is bound to the organised working-class movement, but this link is provided not by the mass of rank-and-file workers, but by the trade union bureaucracy, the apparatus of full-time officials who control the unions. Their influence serves both to root Labour in workers' organisations, and to prevent it playing a revolutionary role.

It was the trade union leaders who set up the Labour Representation Committee in 1900, to provide them with a voice in parliament. It was only in 1918, under the impact of the Russian revolution, that Labour adopted its present constitution, whose famous Clause Four calls for the 'common ownership of the means of production, distribution and exchange'. But the party is to this day dominated by the trade union block vote at conference.

Trade unions are contradictory institutions. On the one hand, they mobilise the collective strength which workers have at the point of production. On the other hand, the trade unions operate *within* the limits of capitalism. They seek, not to overthrow it, but to improve workers' position within the existing system. Their aim is not to end exploitation, but to renegotiate the terms on which workers are exploited. As Marx put it, they deal with effects, not the causes of these effects.

The trade unions, even if they are born out of elemental struggles between labour and capital, inevitably produce a layer of full-time officials whose task it is to negotiate a compromise between these two classes. In Britain this process began as long ago as the 1840s and 1850s, after the defeat of a wave of strikes. Sidney and Beatrice Webb commented that 'during these years we watch a shifting of the leadership in the trade-union world from the casual enthusiast and irresponsible agitator to a class of permanent salaried officers chosen out of the rank and file of trade unionists for their superior business capacity.'

A trade-union official is in a very different position from the workers he represents. He is removed from the discipline of the shopfloor, from its dirt and dangers, from the daily conflicts with foreman and manager, from the fellowship of his workmates. Now he works in an office, and almost certainly earns more than his members do.

Moreover, his earnings no longer depend on the ups and downs of the economy — he no longer has to rely on getting overtime, nor will he be hit by short-time or lay-offs. If he negoti-ates a redundancy agreement, his own job is not at stake. Very often he has not been elected; his appointment may be for life.

Continually involved in negotiations with management, the trade-union official comes to see bargaining, compromise, the reconciliation of labour and capital, as the very stuff of trade unionism. Strikes become a nuisance, disrupting the bargaining process, maybe threatening the union's funds. As Rosa Luxemburg put it: 'the organisation . . . from being a means has gradually changed into an end in itself, a precious thing, to which the interests of the struggles should be subordinated.'

The conservative role played by trade-union officials within the labour movement thus springs from their social position. It isn't a matter of individual trade-union leaders having right-wing views. On the contrary, even if their political beliefs are apparently very left-wing, they will still try to hold back workers in struggle.

The best example of this in Britain was the performance in the 1970s of Jack Jones of the Transport and General Workers Union, and Hugh Scanlon of the Engineers. Dubbed by the press as the 'Terrible Twins' for their militant socialist views when they were elected, Jones and Scanlon turned out to be remarkably moderate in practice. In 1972, a year of the greatest working-class victories since before the General Strike, Scanlon did his best to prevent the wave of engineering factory occupations which swept Manchester, while Jones tried to stop the dockers from taking on the Heath government over the Industrial Relations Act.

Once the Tories had finally been thrown out in the election of 1974, Jones and Scanlon threw all their efforts into supporting the new Labour government, even if that meant sacrificing their own members' interests. The result was three years of wage controls, which led to a marked decline in working-class living standards.

The most flagrant recent example of treachery by trade union leaders is, of course, the 1984–5 miners' strike. The Trades Union Congress in September 1984 pledged its support to the miners, committing its member unions to black the movement of scab coal and oil. Had this policy been observed, then the miners would without doubt have won. Instead all the trade union leaders, including right-wingers such as David Basnett of the General, Municipal and Boilermakers (the key union in the power stations) and left-wingers such as Ron Todd of the Transport and General

Workers' Union, did nothing. This sabotage rendered the miners' eventual defeat almost inevitable.

There is, therefore, a continual conflict within the trade unions between the full-time officials and the rank and file. The trade union bureaucracy is bound, by its position in society, to defend the existing order of things. The trade unions are, as a result, a conservative force within the Labour Party, which has always been run by an alliance of the parliamentary leadership and the big union bosses hostile to radical socialist policies.

Each successive attempt by the left to win control of the Labour Party has therefore been crushed. In 1921 the newly-formed Communist Party was twice refused permission to affiliate. Local Labour Parties which joined the Communist-led National Left-Wing Movement were expelled. Even the moderately left-wing Independent Labour Party despaired of converting Labour to socialism and disaffiliated in 1932 after Labour Prime Minister Ramsay MacDonald had broken away and formed a National Government in collaboration with the Tories.

Some successes were won in the turmoil after MacDonald's betrayal. The 1932 Labour Party Conference defied the National Executive and voted for sweeping nationalisations. But these gains were short-lived, and in 1939 Stafford Cripps, Aneurin Bevan, and other left-wing leaders were expelled.

Cripps was later re-admitted and took a path that was to be followed by later left-wing leaders. In the 1945 Labour government he became Chancellor of the Exchequer, implementing austerity policies which forced down workers' living standards. In October 1946 Cripps declared that 'it would be almost impossible to have worker-controlled industry in Britain, even if it were on the whole desirable.'

The same pattern was repeated in the 1950s. Aneurin Bevan resigned from the Attlee government in April 1951 in protest against a budget massively boosting defence spending and imposing prescription charges in the National Health Service. The Bevanites, as the left came to be called, won considerable support among the constituency parties. Once again, the National Executive clamped down. The Bevanites were forced to give up campaigning among the party rank and file, and Bevan himself narrowly escaped expulsion in 1955. By the 1957 Conference, as shadow Foreign Secretary, he was denouncing unilateral nuclear disarmament as an 'emotional spasm'.

The left-wing revival of recent years has followed the same course. The public sector strikes of the 1978–9 'winter of discontent' and Labour's election defeat in 1979 flung the party into disarray. The left were able to win a series of conference victories thanks to the support of trade-union leaders disgruntled with Labour's performance in office. But the left's advance was based on foundations of sand. The union block vote that had passed their resolutions could as easily be used against them. At the 1982 Conference it was, installing a right-wing National Executive and backing a purge of the Militant tendency.

Since the June 1983 general election this process has gone much further. The Kinnock-Hattersley leadership installed at that year's conference set out to drag the party rightwards. Eighteen months later two left-wing MPs on Labour's national executive, Tony Benn and Eric Heffer, protested at the 'quiet revolution' mounted by the new leadership. They listed the changes, including the abandonment of key left-wing policies — the alternative economic strategy, withdrawal from the Common Market, reductions in defence expenditure — and a stepping up of the purge of Militant supporters and other socialists.

Benn and Heffer, writing in **Tribune** on 31 May 1985, concluded:

> The changes described above . . . represent a far bigger change in the party's constitution than occurred in the 1979–81 period; they take us back to the structure that existed pre-war and post-war when the Parliamentary Labour Party and the general secretaries of some major unions effectively ran the party and the National Executive Committee was weak and ineffective.

This rightward shift was underlined in the autumn of 1985. Kinnock used the TUC and Labour Party conference arrogantly to assert the power of the leader and his right to ignore conference decisions, in the process savagely attacking miners' leader Arthur Scargill and the Militant Tendency.

The most striking feature of this entire process was the way in which Kinnock received the support of most Labour constituency activists. This was the phenomenon of 'Bennism without Benn' — the desertion of the left-wing cause by many of its erstwhile supporters. Within days of the miners' defeat in March 1985 Ken Livingstone had sabotaged the Greater London Council's policy of defying Tory rate-capping legislation and made his peace with Kinnock. Throughout the country members of the Labour Co-ordinating Committee, formed to back Benn in the late 1970s, helped organise the witch-hunt of Militant supporters.

This reflected both long and short-term factors. In the wake of the miners' defeat many Labour left-wingers drew the conclusion that the industrial struggle could not defeat the Tories. The only way they could see of getting rid of Thatcher was by electing a Kinnock government.

There were, however, more fundamental reasons for the collapse of the Labour left. The Labour Party is especially unsuitable terrain for winning support for socialist politics. The reason for the party's existence is to win elections, and its organisation reflects this fact. Constituency and ward parties, as their names suggest, are based on electoral divisions.

Elections break up the working class into a collection of individuals. Each of us votes on our own. It is an individual act. But as individuals we are especially vulnerable to establishment propaganda. We are subject to the barrage of right-wing ideas from television and newspapers.

Elections are supposed to be highly political occasions. In fact the opposite is true. The last thing that politicians want to talk about at election-time is politics. What they want to talk about is votes. And the less you talk about politics the more votes you're likely to win — otherwise, you might offend someone.

Kinnock and his backers are thus being entirely logical. They want to see Labour win elections, and they know that radical socialist policies are vote-losers. So they impose 'moderate' policies on the party.

One of the most insidious things about the Labour Party is how it corrupts those who seek to change it. They may start off hoping for revolutionary change. But gradually they adapt to the environment in which they find themselves.

Political activity comes to mean moving resolutions at ward meetings, or canvassing at election time. Those involved tend to lose touch with ordinary working people. The logic of electoralism, of winning at any cost, comes to prevail.

The radical firebrands end up as safe members of the party establishment — Stafford Cripps, Aneurin Bevan, Michael Foot, and now Ken Livingstone. No doubt they will be followed by others.

This process even affects those Labour Party members who regard themselves as revolutionary socialists. The Militant Tendency is much the largest and most serious socialist grouping inside the Labour Party, and has won the support of many fine working-class activists, especially on Merseyside. But the long haul of operating inside the Labour Party has come to affect Militant's politics, leading its supporters fundamentally to blur the distinction between reform and revolution. Thus Militant's programme declares that 'an entirely peaceful transformation of society is possible in Britain', while its theoretical journal asserts that 'the struggle to establish a socialist Britain can be carried through in parliament, backed up by the colossal power of the labour movement'.

These are more than mere theoretical concessions to parliamentary socialism, as we can see from the experience of Liverpool City Council after a left-wing Labour team, which included Militant supporters, won control in 1983. The council avoided a confrontation with the Tories over its pledge to defend jobs and services in 1984, when they could have fought alongside the miners and opened a second front against Thatcher. Liverpool's Labour leaders accepted a compromise which delayed the crunch for a year. Then, in September 1985, they tried to lay off the entire municipal workforce of 31,000, in an attempt to keep the council financially afloat. This not only made it difficult to win council workers' support against the Tories, but laid Militant open to vicious attack from Kinnock and the Labour right wing.

The Labour Party is a dead end for socialists. More than eighty years have seen a succession of Labour governments which have sometimes succeeded in improving workers' lives but which have left the citadels of capitalist power intact. Nor, as we have seen, can Labour be changed into a fighting socialist party. On the contrary, again and again it is the socialists who have been changed by the party they have joined.

It is time to look for an alternative to Labour. We need socialism more urgently than ever. But it won't come through parliament and the Labour Party.

SOCIALISM FROM BELOW

THE REFORMIST TRADITION sees socialism as something which comes 'from above'. It is to be achieved, *on workers' behalf*, by an enlightened minority — MPs, trade-union leaders, Labour Party activists. 'Leave it to us,' they say. 'All you need do is vote Labour at election time'. The mass of working people are expected to play a purely passive role, just looking on while others transform society for them.

This fits in with how capitalist society is organised. Working people are constantly told — at school, on television, in the press — that they are incompetent. The only people qualified to run society are the experts — the managers, civil servants, politicians, trade-union leaders.

The revolutionary socialist tradition starts from a complete and utter rejection of this arrogant and elitist approach. We stand for socialism 'from below'. Only workers can liberate themselves. No one can do it for them. In Marx's words, socialism is 'the self-emancipation of the working class'.

But what evidence is there that the working class can, and will transform society? Don't workers seem instead to *accept* the existing order, to judge, for example, by their overwhelming rejection of the Labour Party in the 1983 General Election?

To answer these questions we have first to look at *what* gives the workers the power to change the world.

Early critics described capitalism as 'the factory system', and that is the key point. Capitalism brings workers together into large units: factories, mines, offices, hospitals, railway systems. In these units, our labour is organised on a massive scale. Before capitalism, making a table would be the work of one, perhaps two men. Today a furniture company will use the labour of perhaps twenty workers to produce a table — ranging from the forest worker who cuts down the trees, through the designers and joiners, to the spray polishing department and finally the sales assistant. And a table is a fairly simple product. To produce all the hundreds of components that go to make a car or aeroplane, thousands of people are organised to work collectively, co-operating together on a massive scale.

Capitalism organises and exploits workers *collectively*. Our work is organised on the basis of social co-operation and the division of labour. Capitalism has in fact given workers tremendous collective power, power which runs factories, hospitals, schools, transport systems. This power creates all the things that we need as human beings — and often things which we do *not* need, such as weapons of mass destruction, for the capitalist class controls and uses this power for its own ends and its own profit.

But the collective power that is used to run a factory can also be used to stop that factory, and *could* be used to run it in the interests of the workers themselves.

To use their tremendous economic power, workers have to act collectively. Solidarity in going on strike and stopping your workplace is central. But this collective activity, this workers' co-operation on a huge scale, is precisely what capitalism has organised.

How is it then, we may ask, that workers do not use their collective power and simply take over? The reason, of course, is that we are constantly told we are not capable of running things — in school, in the press, on television. The whole current of ideas in society tells us that workers work, following orders handed down from above, and that this is the natural order of things. Slaves used to believe that slavery was natural too.

But there is one point at which workers challenge this order of things — when the collective power that runs factories, offices, hospitals and railways *is* used to stop them. And this is very important. For it means that a strike isn't just something negative.

It isn't just a way of hitting back at the boss, of forcing him to pay higher wages. Every strike, however limited its goal, carries within it the embryo of socialism.

For what is socialism? With the frills removed, it is people collectively running society. Instead of being the prisoners of anarchic capitalist competition and the mad rush for profit at any cost, it is working together for the common good. Our tremendous co-operative power would be controlled, not by a ruling class in the search for ever greater profits, but democratically and for the fulfilment of human need.

Many dismiss socialist ideas as utopian. It's a good idea, they say, but people are too greedy and selfish for it to work in practice. They forget that each and every day we work together co-operatively on a massive scale. They forget too, or perhaps have never been lucky enough to experience, the co-operation and solidarity that are displayed in every strike.

This doesn't mean that strikers set out consciously with social-ist goals in mind. Of course they don't, with very few exceptions. But collective action is the only way to win a strike. The *logic* of workers' position under capitalism — collective action in produc-tion, collective action in struggle — takes us in a socialist direction.

There's another point as well. Workers get involved in strike action for some limited goal, for higher wages or better working conditions. But once involved in struggle, united to achieve a common goal, their ideas can change. At last you're running something for yourself, not just being part of a massive machine run by people above you. This is how workers gain confidence, gain a sense of their ability to control their own lives, their ability to change things.

Strikers also find that their own experience clashes with the dominant ideas in society. It's difficult to believe that the police are a neutral and benevolent force when they break your picket-lines. And you soon stop believing that the unions run the country when you come out on strike.

Workers *change* in struggle, They learn how society is run. They also learn that collective organisation and action can chal-lenge the way society is loaded against them. And they gain confi-dence in themselves. The miners' strike amply showed this: thousands of men and women in the mining communities were transformed by that mammoth struggle.

So socialists, above all, have to be involved in workers'
struggles. For only in struggle can significant numbers of people be
won to socialist politics.

This helps explain why the Labour Party is such an unfavour-
able terrain for socialists. The focus of Labour Party activity is not
workers' struggles, but elections. This means that the Labour
Party does not relate to workers when they are most open to
socialist ideas. To open the road towards socialism, a different sort
of party is needed.

Trade unions and socialism

It is fashionable for some socialists to dismiss the unions as reactionary, 'economistic', interested only in short-term, narrow issues
such as higher wages. Despite the conservative role played by trade-
union officials, we can now see why this attitude is wrong. Every
strike, however limited its objectives, contains the beginnings of
socialism. Through trade-union battles fought over wages, jobs,
hours, and conditions, workers develop the organisation, confidence and consciousness to take on what William Morris called the
'tremendous organisation' of capitalism. For Marx, trade unions
were 'schools of communism', where workers become aware of
their ability to transform society.

Nevertheless, trade unions themselves operate within the
limits of capitalism. They seek to improve the terms on which
workers are exploited, not to destroy the system which exploits
them. As we have seen, this means that the unions are dominated
by a bureaucracy of full-time officials who continually seek to
reconcile the interests of capital and labour, even if this means
betraying their own members.

Workers have responded to the betrayals of the trade-union
bureaucracy in the past by creating their own organisations. These
are bodies controlled by the rank and file through elected lay
delegates, and used by them as a means of fighting independently
of the full-time officials. The classic case in Britain is, of course,
shop stewards' organisation.

By and large, however, shop stewards' organisation is usually
highly fragmented, based on individual workplaces or sections.
But there have been times when offensives by the employers and
the state have forced workers to band together and create such
rank-and-file movements on a national scale. The most famous of

these was the Shop Stewards' and Workers' Control Movement
during the First World War. Its approach was summed up by the
Clyde Workers' Committee in 1915, which stated:

> We will support the officials just so long as they rightly represent the
> workers, but we will act independently immediately they misrepre-
> sent them. Being composed of delegates from every shop and untram-
> melled by obsolete rule of law, we claim to represent the true feeling of
> the workers. We can act immediately according to the merits of the
> case and the desire of the rank and file.

This aspiration to a rank and file united across different trades
and industries has surfaced again and again in the history of the
British labour movement.

But no trade union organisation, however militant, is enough
to defeat capitalism. Trade unions, we are told, are concerned with
economic issues, such as wages and working hours. Politics, however, is quite different. It is to do with winning elections, and that
is the job of a political party — in Britain the Labour Party. A
division of labour operates, with the trade unions fighting on the
economic front, the parliamentary Labour Party on the political
front.

This separation of politics and economics is very damaging. In
reality 'politics is the most concentrated expression of economics',
as Lenin put it. In other words, politics isn't about parliament and
elections, it's about class power. The state exists to defend the
economic system through which workers are exploited. There *is* no
separation of politics and economics.

It follows that trade-union struggle, which limits itself to the
economic field, may achieve a temporary victory, but because the
capitalist class remain in control of the state and the economy, they
can always come back for another round. Defeated in a wave of
strikes, the employers can force up unemployment and so weaken
workers' organisation.

The Polish revolutionary socialist Rosa Luxemburg compared
trade unionism to the labour of Sisyphus, who in Greek legend was
condemned for all time to push a stone up a hill, only to watch it roll
down again. Trade-union struggle may win a battle, but not the
war.

This is true even of rank-and-file organisation. Shop stewards
accept the separation of economics and politics, fighting to improve workers' position within an individual workplace. It is only

when the employers and the state launch a general offensive that rank-and-file organisations are under pressure to link together. When they do link up it is usually under the leadership of revolutionary socialists, such as happened with the Communist Party in the 1920s.

Workers' struggles can deal with the power of the capitalist class only if they break out of the confines of trade unionism. Only by ignoring the division of economics and politics, and making our target the capitalist state can the working class hope to win a lasting victory.

The Mass Strike

To set your sights on defeating, not just an individual employer, but the state, isn't that asking of workers an extraordinary leap — from largely accepting the dreary everyday reality of capitalist society to seeking to free themselves through their own actions?

The answer is that people take this leap, in a small way, all the time. Every strike, however minor, interrupts the daily routine of society. It brings workers into open conflict with their exploiter, and brings them to organise themselves. As such, it is a bridge between merely accepting capitalist society, and openly organising to overthrow it.

Of course, whether strikes fulfil this potential depends largely on the circumstances which surround them. In times of economic prosperity, when employers are making large profits, they can afford to concede large wage increases in response to the threat of strike action, or strike action itself. Workers' militancy can be contained within the framework of the system.

But during slumps such as the present one the capitalist system cannot afford to concede improvements in living standards. The bosses are more likely to demand back what they have already given, and in the United States, 'giveback', when workers accept actual cuts in wages, is now becoming common.

This does not mean that workers will necessarily become more political, or even more militant during times of economic depression. Mass unemployment is as likely to breed defeatism and despair, as recent experience shows. But at a certain stage the anger and frustration that has accumulated through a time of recession and defeat bursts to the surface in a wave of militancy.

Sometimes economic factors may spark this off — for example, if the economy begins to recover, and workers stop being laid off, the greater confidence this confers may precipitate large-scale strikes. This was what happened in America in the mid-1930s, when a mild industrial revival provoked a wave of mass strikes and factory occupations, which led to the unionisation of the big car and steel plants.

At other times, a political crisis may be the spark that sets things alight. France had experienced ten years of right-wing rule and a sharp squeeze of living standards when students clashed with riot police in May 1968. Within days, ten million workers were on strike in the largest general strike in European history.

Whatever the immediate cause, capitalism is liable to experience from time to time explosions of worker militancy which threaten to burst through the barriers of existing working-class organisation. Almost invariably rank-and-file workers find themselves at these times in conflict as much with their own trade-union leaders as with the employers and the state.

May 1968 is a good example. The main trade-union federation in France, the CGT, is controlled by the Communist Party, ostensibly a bitter opponent of the right-wing regime of President de Gaulle. Yet the Communist Party violently attacked the students who had sparked off the strike, and the CGT leaders as quickly as they could signed a pay deal with the government in the hope of getting their members back to work. To their horror, the rank and file rejected the agreement: they wanted more than higher wages — they wanted control of the factories.

The same pattern, of mass strike action turning into a political movement, happened in Poland in the summer of 1980. What sparked off the wave of strikes and occupations was a government decision to increase food prices. But the trade union Solidarity, when it emerged from these struggles, was a political challenge to the Polish state. It threatened to undermine the regime's monopoly of political power.

Mass strikes break down the barrier between economics and politics. It can work in the other direction too: in May 1936 an alliance that included the French Socialist and Communist parties won a general election victory — and French workers responded with a wave of factory occupations through which they sought to translate the political victory into economic gains. In doing so they threatened the very basis of the capitalist order, and the leaders of the alliance rushed to get them back to work so that the separation of politics and economics could be restored.

Any mass strike is a challenge to the capitalist state. It threatens to mobilise workers' economic strength against the capitalist state. This was true of the General Strike of May 1926 in Britain. The trade-union leaders protested that it was a purely industrial dispute, and proclaimed their loyalty to the constitution — but the Tory government knew otherwise. They understood that the strike could succeed only by taking on the state, and they exploited the trade-union leaders' fear of such a confrontation to defeat the strike.

The great miners' strike of 1984–5 also involved an enormous confrontation between workers and the state. Once again the ruling class were far more ruthless and class-conscious than the leaders of the labour movement.

These struggles had something else in common. They were examples of the *bureaucratic* mass strike. They were great class confrontations in which, however, not the rank-and-file workers but the trade-union bureaucracy were in control. This explains why the General Strike was called off so quickly and with such ease by the TUC, and why in 1984 the miners used the methods of mass picketing — which had been decisive in their victory in 1972 — so sparingly.

But there is always the possibility that such a struggle will break out of the leadership's control, will become a genuine mass strike in which the initiative comes from below. The upsurge of May 1968 in France began with a one-day strike called by the CGT union federation which the rank and file spontaneously turned into indefinite factory occupations.

The mass strike carries within it the potential of revolution. This is most obviously true in the case of Russia 1905 and 1917, Germany 1918–23, Spain 1936–7, Hungary 1956, Portugal 1974–5, and Poland 1980–1. In each case, mass workers' movements either toppled, or came close to toppling the existing order. But mass strikes alone cannot bring socialism — as these failures and successes have shown. Something more is needed.

THE REVOLUTIONARY TRADITION

WORKERS' COUNCILS

The power of the capitalist system is not, as we have seen, purely economic. It is also political — through its control of the state machine, the army and the police. It also has power over our ideas — through the education system, newspapers, radio and television.

The failure of reformism lies in the simple fact that this power will ultimately be used even against an elected socialist government. It will be used economically, through the flight of capital, as Harold Wilson's government discovered. It will be used ideologically, to whip up popular hatred of socialists — the treatment meted out recently to Arthur Scargill and the striking miners is only a foretaste of what a left-wing government would suffer. And, in the last instance, it will be used politically, forcibly to crush any serious threat to capitalist control of the economy.

The fundamental question is then whether workers have a power to match that of the capitalist class. As we have seen, such a power exists in the collective organisations which workers build to fight their daily battles with capital.

In the process of production, where the wealth of capitalist society is created, workers have the power to paralyse the entire system. This power, usually employed through the trade unions to renegotiate workers' position *within* capitalism, could be used to overturn existing society.

The *fact* of workers' power is indisputable. In Britain, the miners showed it in 1972 and 1974, when they forced the Tory government into a corner when they tried to impose wage controls, from which they could escape only by fighting — and losing — an election. The 1971 Industrial Relations Act was destroyed by workers' collective action — above all by the threat of a general strike when the five dockers' leaders were jailed in Pentonville in July 1972.

There was another glimpse of workers' power twelve years later, in July 1984, when the dockers joined the miners out on strike. For a few heady days Thatcher tottered on the brink of a mass upheaval which might have swept her away. But the dockers' leaders, officials of the Transport and General Workers' Union, managed to snatch defeat from the jaws of victory, and the strike collapsed, leaving the miners to fight on alone.

Normally, however, this enormous strength is kept within the boundaries of what is regarded as acceptable in capitalist society. The trade unions (or, more especially, their leaders) try to confine themselves to purely economic struggles, and to keep out of politics. But some trade-union struggles burst out of these artificial boundaries. For example, militant picketing challenges the capitalist state. Workers take into their own hands the right to control the movement of goods, and defy the authority of the police and the courts.

When a strike becomes general, embracing different sections of workers, the threat becomes greatest. For during a general strike, when the entire economy is paralysed, strike committees are forced to take on the responsibility for running certain essential services, such as ambulances and making sure that food is distributed. In other words, workers' organisations begin to take over some of the functions of the state. This began to happen in Britain during the General Strike of May 1926. In some areas Councils of Action set up by local trade unionists became effectively government bodies.

The General Strike lasted only nine days, but in other countries things have developed much more dramatically. Situations of *dual power* have emerged, where the institutions of the existing capitalist state have been confronted by the beginnings of a rival workers' state.

The first example of this was the Paris Commune. In March 1871 the workers of Paris set up their own government. The most important action they took was to dissolve the standing army and the police, and to replace them with a people's militia. All officials were directly elected, and paid the average workers' wages. Moreover, they were subject to immediate recall — in other words, if the voters decided that they didn't like what one of their representatives was doing, they could vote to remove him.

The Paris Commune was crushed by the French government, and 20,000 men and women were slaughtered for their part in it. But they left behind them the model of what a workers' state would be like. All previous states had been the means through which a minority of exploiters held on to their wealth and power. The workers' state would be the instrument through which working people liberated themselves.

The 'Commune-State' re-emerged in Russia during the revolutions of 1905 and 1917. But now things were taken a step further. For the 1905 revolution gave birth to a form of political organisation which reflected workers' power in production — the *soviet*.

'Soviet' is the Russian word for 'council'. The soviet first emerged in St Petersburg in October 1905 as a council of factory delegates. Formed first as a strike committee by print-workers who wanted to be paid for the punctuation marks as well as the words which they set up into type, it grew into a body which represented all the workers of the city. It cut across all the sectional lines which trade unions reflected, and based itself on the power of workplace organisation.

The 1905 revolution was crushed, but the soviets reappeared on a mass scale when the revolution of February 1917 toppled Tsar Nicholas II. This time these councils included not only the workers but also the millions of soldiers who had rebelled against Russia's involvement in the First World War. Because of this, the soviets directly challenged the ultimate source of state power — the monopoly of armed force. Not only did the councils command the active support of many soldiers, but they created their own workers' militia, the Red Guard. The Provisional Government which replaced the Tsar found itself confronted by what was effectively a workers' government, and one that was growing in strength day by day.

A situation of dual power is unstable — it can't last for any length of time. Either the capitalist class will move against the workers' councils to restore their monopoly of force, or the councils will overthrow the state and take power for themselves. In October 1917 the soviets, led by the Bolsheviks, seized power from the Provisional Government.

The October revolution was only the high-point of a wave of workers' militancy which shook Europe from one corner to another. In Germany workers' and soldiers' councils overturned the Kaiser in November 1918. Italy was shaken by two years of class struggle in 1918–20, coming to a climax in the factory occupations of the summer of 1920. Even in Britain the shop stewards' movement represented a serious threat to the government and the trade-union leaders.

We shall look more closely later at the reasons for the success or failure of different workers' movements. It's important to see, however, that the upheavals at the end of the First World War were not a flash in a pan, something unique to those few years and never to be repeated.

In June 1936 the Spanish right wing, led by General Franco, launched a coup d'état against Spain's republican government. It was beaten off by an enormous effort on the part of Spain's workers and peasants, who rose in arms against Franco's professional soldiers. George Orwell, who served in a left-wing militia during the Civil War which followed, wrote this vivid description of Barcelona under workers' control:

> It was the first time I had ever been to a town where the working class was in the saddle. Practically every building of any size had been seized by the workers and was draped with red flags or the red and black flags of the Anarchists; every wall was scrawled with the hammer and sickle and with the initials of the revolutionary parties; almost every church had been gutted and its images burnt. Churches here and there were being systematically demolished by gangs of workmen. Every shop and cafe had an inscription saying that it had been collectivised; even the boot-blacks had been collectivised and their boxes painted red and black. Waiters and shop-walkers looked you in the face and treated you as an equal. Service and even ceremonial forms of speech had temporarily disappeared . . . Tipping was forbidden by law.
> There was much in it that I did not understand, in some ways I did not

even like it, but I recognised it immediately as a state of affairs worth fighting for.

Franco eventually won the Civil War, in part because, on the republican side, these beginnings of a workers' government were suppressed and replaced by an orthodox capitalist regime. But the same pattern of workers' councils re-emerged again in Hungary in 1956, when the mass of the people rebelled against the brutal rule of Moscow and its Hungarian puppet government. Factory councils and an armed workers' militia led the resistance to the Russian tanks which eventually crushed the rising.

In Portugal, when the coup of 23 April 1974 ended nearly fifty years of right-wing dictatorship, the popular upsurge that followed saw the spread of a movement for workers' control of the factories in alliance with rank-and-file soldiers radicalised by the revolution. Although the right wing eventually restored control, the Portuguese events showed the potential for workers' power in Western Europe itself.

Most recently, and most dramatically, when Solidarity emerged in Poland during the summer of 1980 it went much further than a purely trade-union movement. Organising the mass of Polish workers independently of the institutions of the state, it directly threatened the power of the ruling class and its Russian backers. For a time, the regime was forced to concede victory after victory to the workers' movement.

But the case of Solidarity also shows how unstable any situation with elements of dual power is. Just because its very existence represented a direct challenge to the Polish state, Solidarity had to overthrow that state or itself perish. The fact that Lech Walesa and its other leaders insisted on seeking to improve workers' conditions only within the framework of the existing system made them vulnerable to the regime's counter-attack.

While the rest of the Polish state had been badly shaken by the emergence of Solidarity, the armed forces, the ultimate source of any state's power, had survived intact, and could be used to crush the union in December 1981.

The Revolutionary Party

So although workers' struggles may spontaneously throw up soviets or workers' councils, and create a situation of dual power, these conditions are not enough for a successful socialist revolution.

A revolutionary situation places a premium on effective organisation and leadership. Events move very quickly, and on a snap decision may hang the fate of the entire revolution. What is needed is a cool and clear head, a firm sense of the ultimate objective, the ability to make rapid tactical judgements, and an organisation capable not only of making decisions, but of carrying them out.

Unfortunately, none of these qualities are to be found in the leaders of the reformist parties. Yet experience shows that it is they who at first dominate the workers' councils. Even when workers break from the past by creating such councils, they still carry with them many traditions, and especially loyalty to those who have led them in the past. Thus in Russia in February 1917 the two main reformist parties, the Mensheviks and Social Revolutionaries, had a majority in the soviets. Similarly, workers' and soldiers' councils which emerged in Germany in November 1918 were controlled by the reformist Social Democrats and Independent Socialists.

These two revolutions had very different outcomes. In Germany capitalist rule was restored, in the form of the Weimar republic. In Russia, on the other hand, the soviets seized power in the first and only successful workers' revolution. The cause of this difference lies in the simple fact that in Russia a revolutionary socialist party existed at the beginning of the revolution, while in Germany it did not.

The Bolsheviks were founded in 1903, when Lenin and the majority of the Russian Social Democratic Labour Party decided to build an organisation of those who wanted to work for a socialist revolution. The Bolsheviks took part in the revolution of 1905, and nearly fell apart after it was defeated. But a core held together around Lenin, and kept an organisation going during the difficult years between 1906 and 1912. When an upsurge in Russian workers' struggles began with the angry response to a massacre of miners at Lena in 1912, the Bolsheviks were ready, and their semi-legal paper **Pravda** won a wide audience among workers.

This organisation was able to survive the repression which followed the outbreak of the First World War in August 1914, and to give a voice to the growing workers' opposition to the war and the Tsar which exploded into the revolution of February 1917.

The Bolsheviks were, at first, only a minority in the soviets of 1917. But under Lenin's leadership they set themselves the task of

winning the workers' and soldiers' councils to the goal of overthrow-
ing the Provisional Government. They rejected the idea of seizing
power with only minority support, and concentrated on, in Lenin's
words, 'patiently explaining' the need for a second revolution.

The Bolsheviks' arguments, and their own experience, con-
vinced Russian workers of the necessity of this revolution. By the
late summer and early autumn of 1917 the Bolsheviks had a majority in the soviets. After a prolonged internal debate, Lenin persuaded the party to seize power, and on 25 October 1917 the
Provisional Government was overthrown.

Compare what happened in Germany. The revolutionary left
there had in Rosa Luxemburg as outstanding a leader as Lenin.
What they lacked was a party. Rosa Luxemburg and her supporters
in the Spartacus League remained part of the reformist Social
Democratic Party even after it had supported the First World War.
They left only when they were expelled in 1917. Luxemburg then
founded the German Communist Party, on the Bolshevik model,
in December 1918, *after* the revolution had broken out.

This was too late. The reformists dominated the workers' and
soldiers' councils. The Social Democratic premier, Friedrich Ebert,
struck a deal with General Groener of the General Staff to crush the
revolutionary left. Tens of thousands of workers had been radicalised by the revolution but lacked any effective leadership. It was
easy for the right wing to provoke an unsuccessful revolutionary
rising in January 1919 and then slaughter the Spartacists. Luxemburg was the chief victim of this massacre, even though she opposed
the rising.

The same pattern has been repeated again and again since
1918–19. Let's just take the most recent case, that of Poland in
1980–1. The Polish workers were prepared to take action against
the regime and set up their own independent organisation, Solidarity. They were still, however, heavily influenced by the past.

The most important of these influences was the Catholic
Church, the one institution in Poland independent of the state.
Lech Walesa and the 'moderate' wing of the Solidarity leadership
were largely guided by the advice they received from the church,
which said they should seek a compromise with the regime. Unfortunately, within Solidarity there was no revolutionary organisation
capable of presenting a coherent alternative based on the strength
of the working class to overthrow the state. Walesa's strategy led,

as every reformist strategy must, to defeat.

A revolutionary party is a necessary condition of any success-ful revolution. But it's important to understand what a revolution-ary party is, and what it is not.

In the first place, the party is no substitute for the working class itself. The baneful influence of Stalin's perversion of Marx-ism (of which more in the next chapter) has meant that the idea of 'The Party' casts up images of an infallible, all-seeing monolith which makes the revolution *for* the working class.

Such a conception of the party is, of course, completely at odds with Marx's idea of socialism as the self-emancipation of the work-ing class. It is the spontaneous action of workers which creates revolutionary situations with the potential for socialism. What the party seeks to do is to render this movement conscious, and to direct its energies to the goal of wresting power from the capitalist class.

In the words of Leon Trotsky, who was with Lenin the main leader of the Bolshevik revolution: 'Without a guiding organisation the energy of the masses would dissipate like steam not enclosed in a piston-box. But what moves things is not the piston or the box, but the steam.'

Secondly, revolutionaries do not, even in revolutionary situ-ations, spend their time running around with guns and bombs. Their task is rather 'patiently to explain' to workers the necessity of revolution. The chief battle they fight is one of *ideas*, the struggle to break the hold of the past, of conservative traditions on the major-ity of workers.

The revolutionary socialist party does not engage in this battle only through meetings and newspaper articles. As we have seen earlier, workers become open to socialist ideas chiefly when in-volved in struggle. So revolutionaries must involve themselves in the daily trade-union struggles in every workplace, in factory and office, mine and hospital, even though these struggles have very non-revolutionary aims, such as higher wages or better working conditions.

The revolutionary party, in other words, is a *combat* organisa-tion. It does not exist only to discuss ideas, but to engage in, and organise working-class actions. By taking an active part in winning small gains today, revolutionary socialists win the confidence of their fellow-workers, who will then be more likely to see that socialism offers a positive alternative for the future.

Thirdly, the tasks of the party are reflected in its internal organisation. The image of the Bolsheviks which we have inherited, thanks to the degeneration of the Russian revolution, is that of a monolith guided by an infallible leader, Lenin. Nothing could be further from the truth. Before, during and after the October revolution the Bolshevik party was continually engaged in the most vigorous debates, which were often conducted openly in the press, and in which Lenin was often in a minority.

Such lively internal democracy is essential to a revolutionary party. For if it is to intervene in and influence workers' struggles it has continually to be learning from these struggles, and adjusting to changes in circumstances. This can happen only if the party's organisation permits open and democratic debate.

But the other side to this is that the party must be able to intervene effectively in day-to-day workers' struggle. This means that a decision, once arrived at democratically, must be carried out by all the members of the party, even those who were in the minority that opposed the decision. The effectiveness of a revolutionary party lies in the fact that all its members act as one.

This delicate balance — the fullest possible democracy in making a decision, the fullest possible unanimity in carrying it out — is what Lenin called *democratic centralism*. It is essential to the success of a revolutionary socialist party.

There is one final lesson to be drawn from the experience of previous revolutions. The task of building a revolutionary party must begin long *before* a revolutionary situation develops. It was not superior intelligence or courage that distinguished Lenin from Rosa Luxemburg, but simply the fact that he had grasped the need for a party as long ago as 1903, while she broke with the reformist Social Democrats at the last possible moment. As a result, the Bolsheviks had the experience and strength from fourteen years of ups and downs in the workers' movement, while the Spartacists were a weak, divided and disorganised group, highly vulnerable to the counter-offensive.

This has obvious implications for what socialists do today. It is not enough to stagnate in the Labour Party, saying that there will be time enough to break with the right-wing leadership when there is an upturn in the class struggle. We must build an independent revolutionary socialist party *now*, however difficult and discouraging the circumstances may be.

WHY THE 'SOCIALIST' COUNTRIES AREN'T SOCIALIST

RUSSIA — WHAT WENT WRONG

The most powerful single objection to socialism is, without a doubt, the fate of the Russian revolution. 'Go back to Russia,' socialists are constantly told. And indeed there is a case to answer. What is there to stop another successful workers' revolution ending up in a tyranny like Stalin's?

To answer this question, we must look at the historical circumstances in which the Russian revolution took place. Russia was still, at the turn of the nineteenth century, a backward, primarily agricultural country. The bulk of the population were peasants, ruthlessly exploited by the landowning gentry, backed up by the Tsarist state.

In the 1890s the government began to encourage the industrialisation of Russia, fearing that otherwise the country would fall back in the arms race with more advanced powers. An alliance of the state and foreign capital began to build up industry. As a result, a small, but economically and politically powerful industrial working class emerged in the main centres.

The 1905 revolution reflected the explosive impact made by the new working class on the Russian political scene. However, the

Tsarist regime retained control of its vast army of peasant con-
scripts, and so was able to crush the revolution. But in 1917 the
soldiers themselves, under the pressure of military defeat and
workers' revolts, brought down the Tsar.

The Bolsheviks were able to take power in October 1917
because not only did they have the support of the industrial working class, but theirs was the only party to call for an immediate end
to the war, and to support the peasants' right to land. The peasants
were seizing the land anyway, but once the Bolsheviks took power
they legalised these seizures.

The rulers of Western capitalism did not take the October
revolution lying down. No fewer than 22 armies invaded Russia in
an effort to crush the Bolshevik regime. For nearly three years the
country was gripped by a civil war between the new soviet republic
and the armies of the counter-revolutionary Whites and their
Western backers.

Millions of people perished from war, disease and starvation in
these years. The effect of the war on industry was shattering.
Starved of markets and raw materials, the factories closed down.
Those workers who were not sucked into the Red Army or the civil
service returned to the villages from which they came, for there was
no food to be got in the towns. The industrial working class, on
which the Bolsheviks had based their strength, disintegrated.

The Bolsheviks, when they finally emerged victorious from
the civil war in 1921, found themselves in a precarious position.
The disappearance of the working class left them suspended in air,
controlling the state machine but lacking a social base. The peasants had supported them against the Whites, who they feared
would bring back the old landowners, but were becoming increasingly hostile as a result of the Bolsheviks' practice of seizing grain
to feed the towns.

In the spring of 1921 Lenin introduced the 'New Economic
Policy', which to some degree restored the private market as a way
of encouraging the peasants to produce more food. This gave the
Bolshevik regime a breathing space, but it did not resolve its basic
dilemma.

Lenin and Trotsky had never believed that a Russian soviet
republic could survive on its own. They expected the October
revolution to spark off a wave of revolutions in the advanced
capitalist countries of the West. They argued that no single country,

especially one as backward as Russia, could build socialism on its own: this would require the pooled resources of all the major countries.

In line with this strategy, the Bolsheviks launched the Communist International (Comintern) in 1919. Its purpose was to organise world revolution, and to create an international soviet republic. To this end, it set about building new Communist Parties all over the world.

The revolutionary wave which followed the end of the First World War showed that the Bolsheviks' strategy was realistic. The years 1918–20 saw revolution in Germany, soviet republics in Hungary and Bavaria, mutinies and a police strike in Britain, factory occupations in Italy. But the success of the workers' revolution in Russia did not spread to other countries. The fundamental reason for this was the absence of effective revolutionary parties other than the Bolsheviks. By the time that the Comintern was launched, the most favourable conditions for revolution in western and central Europe had for the most part passed. The failure of the German Communist Party to seize power in October 1923 apparently closed the doors to world revolution for the time being.

That, at any rate, was the conclusion drawn by a majority of the Bolshevik leadership. By the time of Lenin's death in January 1924 the party was very different from the workers' organisation it had been in 1917. As the democratic soviets had withered with the destruction of the working class in civil war, so too the Communist Party of the Soviet Union, as the Bolsheviks were now known, had fallen under the control of a bureaucracy of full-time officials.

The head of this bureaucracy was Josef Stalin, the party's general secretary. In the years after Lenin's death he was able gradually to defeat rival after rival, till by 1928 he reigned supreme.

Stalin's importance lay as the representative of the new party-state bureaucracy which now controlled the Soviet Union. These officials were no longer interested in world revolution. Rather, their chief concern was with the interests of the Soviet state, and of themselves as its rulers. In line with this, Stalin and his immediate supporters coined the doctrine of 'socialism in one country'. They argued that it would be possible to build a socialist society within the confines of the Soviet Union alone. The task of the Communist parties in other countries was not to make the revolution, but to further the interests of the Russian state. The Comintern was 'bolshevised', its national sections transformed into agents of the Russian foreign office.

This abandonment of world revolution was a self-fulfilling prophecy. Again and again in the years between 1923 and 1939, Moscow's orders led local Communist Parties into disastrous defeats. The two most important of these were in China and Germany.

The Chinese revolution of 1925–27 saw millions of workers and peasants battling against the foreign powers which were exploiting China, and against their local allies. But Stalin, eager for a friendly neighbour country, instructed the Chinese Communist Party to support the Kuomintang, led by Chiang Kai-shek, which hoped to build a Western-style capitalist regime in China. The result was that, once the Communists had served their purpose and the war was won, Chiang turned on them and slaughtered tens of thousands of workers and peasants.

In Germany the Communist Party had the support of millions of workers, although the reformist Social Democratic Party still dominated the labour movement. The Great Depression, when it broke out in 1929, led to a rapid increase in support for Hitler's Nazis. The Communists, on Stalin's orders, refused to form an alliance with the Social Democrats to stop the Nazis. Instead they said that the Social Democrats — the equivalent of the British Labour Party — were as bad as the Nazis, calling them 'social fascists'. These divisions enabled Hitler to come to power in January 1933. The most powerful labour movement in the world submitted to fascism with barely a whimper.

These catastrophes increased Russia's isolation from the rest of the world. Confronted with the capitalist world system, any socialist regime has two choices. It can either seek to overthrow it by encouraging revolutionary movements in other countries, or it can adapt to that system, conforming to its laws. Russia's rulers had rejected the first alternative when they adopted the doctrine of 'socialism in one country'. The logic of their position was that they had increasingly to act like a capitalist great power.

Even before Hitler's victory the Soviet Union was threatened militarily by the West. To meet this threat the Russian state needed a powerful military establishment of its own. Since the technology of modern warfare depends on heavy industry, the Soviet bureaucracy under Stalin set out to build up this heavy industry from scratch.

As Stalin put it: 'To slacken the pace [of industrialisation] would mean to lag behind; and those who lag behind are beaten. We do not want to be beaten . . . We are fifty or a hundred years behind the advanced countries. We must make good this lag in ten years. Either we do so or they crush us.'

From 1928 onwards Stalin's Russia embarked on a programme of forced industralisation designed to catch up with the West. Within ten years an enormous range of heavy industries had been built up. But the price of this great economic advance had been paid by the mass of workers and peasants.

Forced to rely on their own resources, Russia's rulers could industrialise only by exploiting their working population. They needed to import machinery from the West. The only way in which they could finance these imports was through selling grain abroad. But grain was produced by the peasantry, who were reluctant to hand it over to the West. So Stalin collectivised agriculture, seizing the land from the peasants and forcing them into state-run collective farms. Millions perished in the process, and Russian agriculture still has to recover from its effects.

A similar story can be told of Russian industry. The remaining gains made by workers during the revolution were wiped out. The trade unions were transformed into instruments of management. Piece-rates were introduced, so that workers had to make greater and greater efforts to earn a basic wage. A Russian economist has calculated that the industrialisation of the 1930s was financed by a huge increase in the exploitation of the working class.

By the time Hitler invaded Russia in 1941, the Russian state had become a strong enough industrial power eventually to repel the German armies. But Russian society had been transformed. The vastly increased industrial working class had no more control over the economy than workers did in the West. Although legally the means of production were owned by the state, in reality they were controlled by the party-state bureaucracy. A new ruling class had formed among the ruins of the soviets.

The process had been a bloody one. Stalin, according to his successor, Nikita Krushchev, was responsible for the death of twelve million people. Among them were most of the old Bolshevik Party, who perished during the Great Purges launched in 1936. Millions of people were arrested by Stalin's secret police, and disappeared into the great system of labour camps in Siberia. Most never returned.

The slaughter enabled Stalin to eliminate any vestiges of the workers' state created in October 1917. But what sort of society had replaced that state? Clearly, it was, and continues to be, a class society. The top of the Russian bureaucracy and their families enjoy a privileged existence, quite removed from ordinary working people. The great wave of strikes in 1980 and 1981 which shook Poland, a society very similar to Russia, revealed the privileges of this new ruling class — their special hospitals and schools, luxury villas and Swiss bank accounts.

What makes these societies tick? Despite their apparent differences from Western capitalist countries, the basic pattern is very similar. We saw that capitalism involves accumulation. In other words, capitalists constantly reinvest profits in further production. The same is true of the Soviet Union. The goal of production is not the needs of the mass of the people. On the contrary, their living standards are much lower than our own. Instead, resources are constantly poured into building up heavy industry. Consumption is sacrificed to production.

Why do the Russian ruling class do this? For exactly the same reason as capitalists accumulate in the West. *Because of competition.* Except that in Russia's case the competition is less economic than military. The Soviet state is under constant pressure to keep up a military establishment comparable to that of the United States. This is an enormous burden for an economy half the size of the US and with much lower productivity. So some 15 per cent of gross national product is devoted to defence spending. Everything else is sacrificed to keep up in the arms race.

This is exactly the same sort of arrangement that we find in Western capitalism. There firms are forced to reinvest their profits because if they don't they will be forced out of business by their rivals. Russia is forced to concentrate on building up heavy industry because otherwise she will be wiped out by America.

The only difference is that while it is firms that compete in Western capitalism, the arms race takes place between states. What we have in Russia is *state* capitalism. The state owns the economy, and the central political bureaucracy runs the state. It is they who form the capitalist class in Russia.

Anyone who doubts this should look at what has happened in Eastern Europe in the past thirty years. After the Second World

War the Russians seized military control of Eastern Europe and used their armed might to transform these countries into state-capitalist societies.

The result has been wave after wave of working-class revolts against the local ruling class and their backers in Moscow — Berlin 1953, Hungary and Poland 1956, Czechoslovakia 1968, Poland 1971, 1976 and 1980–81. If these countries really are socialist, run in the interests of the working class, why has it so often been necessary for workers to rebel against them?

In conclusion, it's important to stress that this degeneration of the Russian revolution wasn't inevitable. Things could have happened differently. If the revolution had spread from Russia to the advanced industrial countries after 1917, then the horrors of Stalin's rule would have been avoided and the working class would have held on to power.

Even after the first revolutionary wave had receded, there was an alternative to the course eventually followed. Leon Trotsky and the Left Opposition in Russia argued that the Bolshevik Party should continue to concentrate on encouraging revolutions in other countries. Had that advice been followed, then the Chinese and German disasters might have been averted, and the history of the twentieth century would then have been very different.

As it was, the Left Opposition was crushed, expelled from the party, and imprisoned or driven into exile. Nevertheless, they kept the cause of revolutionary socialism alive. They served as a reminder that Stalin was the antithesis of Marx and Lenin, that what he achieved was the destruction of socialism, not the fulfilment of the dreams of those who made the revolution of 1917.

Revolution in the Third World

The Russian revolution was the first, and greatest of the revolutions of the twentieth century. The others that followed it have taken place chiefly in what is now called the Third World, the poor and backward countries of Asia, Africa, and Latin America. The most important of these revolutions, China, Vietnam and Cuba, all claim to be socialist, and to some degree to have modelled themselves on the Russian example. How much truth is there in this claim?

The first thing to remember is that all these revolutions were directed against colonial, or semi-colonial exploitation. China had been dismembered and humiliated by foreign powers in the nineteenth century; Vietnam was a French colony; Cuba was effectively controlled by American capital.

The great achievements of the Third World revolutions have been as movements of national liberation. Foreign exploiters were expelled, and national independence achieved. In general the standard of living of the peoples of the countries concerned has risen as a result of these revolutions. In these respects, the revolutions were undoubtedly progressive developments which deserved the support of socialists everywhere.

But they weren't socialist revolutions, nor are the regimes they have produced socialist. This is most obvious when we look at who was involved in the revolutions. What is striking is how small a part was played by the industrial working class.

For example, the Chinese revolution of 1925–27 was undoubtedly an upheaval in which the labour movement played a central role. But thanks to the bad advice given to the Chinese Communists by Stalin, the revolution was defeated and the labour movement destroyed. Driven from the towns, the Chinese Communists took refuge in the countryside. Under the leadership of Mao Tse-tung they perfected a strategy of guerrilla warfare based on the peasantry.

Once the Japanese had destroyed the Kuomintang regime of Chiang Kai-shek, only themselves to be defeated by the allies during the Second World War, Mao's peasant armies were able to seize the initiative. They launched an offensive which resulted in the Communist seizure of the country in 1949. The urban working class were reduced, in this struggle, to the status of passive observers.

The Vietnamese Communist Party, in its epic forty-five years struggle for national independence, similarly relied on peasant guerrilla forces. Fidel Castro's 26 July Movement in Cuba had a much narrower base, being composed largely of middle-class intellectuals. A similar pattern has been repeated in many other countries — Angola, Mozambique, Zimbabwe, Nicaragua, where intellectuals have led largely peasant armies. The 'socialist' rulers of Ethiopia came to power as a result of a military coup!

The importance of this lies in the fact that the peasantry are a very different sort of class from the working class. They tend to be small-holders, each household owning or renting its own small plot of land and working it on their own. Therefore, they are isolated from each other and do not have the collective, co-operative strength of industrial workers organised in production and in trade unions.

This means that when peasants rebel, as they have throughout history, their horizons tend to be very narrow. They will seize control of their landlord's estate and divide it among themselves. But they are unlikely to worry about events outside their village, and so are very vulnerable to the centralised power of the state.

Peasants form *national* movements only under the leadership of another class. During the Great French Revolution of 1789 that class was the capitalists, who used the peasants to break the power of the monarchy and the landed aristocracy. In Russia 1917 it was the working class who led the peasants. This reflected the weakness of the Russian capitalist class, which was too dependent on the Tsarist state and foreign capital, and too afraid of the working class, to take part in any revolutionary struggle.

In the Third World in the era of the colonial revolutions, both capitalist and working classes were weak. The capitalists were too bound up with the colonial powers to act as an independent force. The workers were a minority of the population without revolutionary class organisations. Neither workers nor capitalists were therefore able to lead the peasants in their battle for freedom from foreign exploitation.

This vacuum was filled by the educated middle classes. This group — schoolteachers, civil servants, lawyers and journalists — had been encouraged by the colonial state to aspire to the same status as their foreign masters. At the same time, racism meant that educated natives were denied the positions to which their qualifications entitled them. The anger and humiliation which this caused pushed middle-class intellectuals into political activity.

Often the middle classes joined the Communist Party. But people like Mao Tse-tung and his Vietnamese counterpart Ho Chi Minh saw themselves as nationalists first, and socialists second. Their aim was national independence. They admired Stalin's Russia because it seemed to have succeeded in building up a strong national economy, not because it had anything to do with workers' power.

The nationalist aspirations of the colonial revolutionary leaders are reflected in the regimes they created. In all essentials they were replicas of Russian state capitalism. Most economic activity of any importance was placed under state control, while the party controlled the state. Effective power was in the hands of the central political bureaucracy. Workers and peasants might, at best, enjoy some power at a local level: they had no control over the central government or the levers of the national economy.

To understand the colonial revolutions, it is best to compare them, not with Russia in 1917, but with an earlier wave of revolutions — England 1640, America 1776, France 1789. Marx called these bourgeois revolutions. Their aim was to sweep away feudalism and absolute monarchy, and so create the conditions in which capitalism could prosper and develop.

The Third World revolutions were also bourgeois revolutions, but taking place in very different conditions. Their target was not the overthrow of feudalism, but the destruction of colonialism. In a world economy dominated by a handful of Western capitalist powers, Mao, Ho, Castro, and the many who have tried to emulate them, sought to create strong and independent nation-states. State capitalism, by concentrating all resources in the hands of the government, seemed to be the only way of attaining their objective.

But if they have achieved national independence, they have not succeeded in separating themselves from the pressures of the world economy. China under Mao sought to break away in a much more radical way than Stalin's Russia had ever attempted. Rather than rely on Western technology, the Chinese Communist Party decided to use only their own resources. The most important of these was the Chinese people themselves. The Cultural Revolution of the late 1960s was intended to mobilise the energy and enthusiasm of the working masses behind the goal of building an independent national economy.

But this strategy failed because of the sort of military pressures which had forced Russia under Stalin to industrialise. Only in this case, ironically, the military threat came from China's fellow so-called 'socialist' country, Russia. Armed clashes on the border between Russia and China in early 1969 forced the Chinese leadership to abandon the Cultural Revolution.

Since that time, despite a number of brief U-turns, they have sought to build up Chinese industry by using Western capital and technology. This has led them to encourage foreign investment in China, and increasingly to push its products on the international market (Chinese textile exports are the fastest growing in the world). It has even been announced recently that China will start investing in projects abroad. If you can't beat 'em, join 'em.

The power of the world system has also been felt by other state-capitalist regimes. Cuba under Castro sought to end her almost exclusive dependence on sugar exports. Yet all she has succeeded in doing is to make Russia, rather than the US, the main recipient of her sugar. Heavily dependent on Russian subsidies, Castro is also deeply in debt to the Western banks.

The goal of building independent national economies has turned out to be an unattainable dream. Every country, like it or not, is a part of the capitalist world-system, and is subject to its pressures. This is as true of those Third World states which have allied themselves to the West, as it is of China, Cuba and their like.

For example, Brazil was the great economic miracle of the 1960s and 1970s. Even during the first world slump in the mid-1970s her economy continued to grow rapidly. Sao Paolo swelled into the largest industrial conurbation in Latin America, with a population of thirteen million producing more than most countries in the continent.

The miracle, however, had been based on borrowing enormous amounts of money from Western banks. When the second slump hit the world in 1980, Brazil found herself heavily in debt to the West, while at the same time her export markets were shrinking because of the recession. The government was forced to turn to the International Monetary Fund. As a price for not calling in Brazil's 90 billion dollar debts, the IMF and the Western banks demanded tough austerity policies — heavy cuts in workers' living standards and widespread sackings.

No state can escape from the world system. The only way out is an international socialist revolution. One of the most important harbingers of that revolution is the growth of the industrial working class in the Third World. For example, in Brazil since 1964 the number of industrial workers has more than trebled, to twelve million. In recent years they have begun to flex their muscles, above all in a series of carworkers' strikes which have forced Brazil's shaken military rulers to make major political concessions.

A similar story could be told of other countries — South Korea, Egypt, Argentina, South Africa, Bolivia. The working class will be centrally involved in any future upheavals in the Third World.

The Western Communist Parties

The Russian example has not been a model only for the Third World. The revolution of 1917 was an inspiration to millions of workers throughout Europe who flocked to join the Communist Parties after the foundation of the Comintern in 1919.

Although in their earlier years these parties were genuine revolutionary socialist organisations, by the late 1920s they had been transformed into instruments of the Russian bureaucracy. Communist Party leaders in the West became Moscow's appointees. If they failed to fall into line with every twist and turn of the Kremlin, they would be dismissed, disgraced, expelled, even murdered. It was on Stalin's orders that, as we have seen, the Communist Parties pursued strategies which led to the defeat of the Chinese revolution of 1925–27 and to Hitler's triumph in Germany.

In 1935, after the German catastrophe, the Comintern adopted the Popular Front strategy which still forms the basis of Western Communist Party practice today. The strategy was chosen for reasons of Russian foreign policy. Stalin hoped to prevent a German Nazi invasion of Russia through an alliance with the 'democratic' capitalist powers, Britain, France, and America.

The Popular Front was designed to achieve this end. The Communist parties should unite against fascism, not just with the Social-Democrats and Labour Parties, but also with 'democratic' capitalists opposed to fascism. This strategy amounted to an abandonment of the goal of socialist revolution. For capitalists, however liberal, would always be opposed to the confiscation of their own property. Therefore, in practice, the Communist Parties had to hold back workers' struggles in order to prevent them from antagonising the capitalist parties involved in the Popular Front.

In France the Popular Front embraced the Socialists, Communists, and the Radicals, the main capitalist party. Swept to office in the 1936 elections, the Popular Front government of Leon Blum found itself faced, even before it was formed, by a wave of mass strikes and factory occupations. Fearful that this display of working-class power would break up the Popular Front, French Communist leader Maurice Thorez announced that 'It is necessary to know when to end a strike', and persuaded the workers to end their actions.

After that it was downhill all the way. Blum implemented some reforms, but found further advance blocked by his Radical partners. Eventually he abandoned office, and his successors moved gradually to the right. The parliament elected with a Popular Front majority in 1936 and the full support of the left voted to power the fascist Vichy regime after France's defeat by Hitler in 1940.

The consequences of the Popular Front strategy were even more disastrous in Spain. When General Franco led a military rebellion against Spain's Popular Front government in 1936 he was stopped only by a virtual workers' and peasants' revolution. In the civil war that followed, the Republican government's main ally was Stalin's Russia, while fascist Germany and Italy poured in arms and men on Franco's side.

Stalin, however, was afraid of antagonising Britain and France. So the Communist Party devoted all its efforts to pushing back the frontiers of the revolution — replacing the workers' and peasants' militia with a professional army, restoring seized factories and estates to their owners, and murdering revolutionary activists. But once the revolution had been strangled, there was little left to fight for. In 1939 the surviving Republican areas succumbed to Franco's armies.

The slaughter of the First World War had led to a wave of socialist ideas and workers' revolts throughout Europe. In 1945, as the Second World War ended, a similar wave of radicalism again swept Europe. Could socialism again have been on the agenda? But for Stalin the answer would have been yes.

The Comintern had been dissolved by Stalin in 1943 to re-assure Russia's Western allies of his conservative intentions. In Britain and the US, the Communist Party had held back workers' struggle, opposing strikes because they undermined the war effort. In many countries Communists had led the resistance to German occupation. By the end of the war there were Communist-controlled partisan armies in France, Italy, Greece, Belgium, Yugoslavia, and Czechoslovakia.

But Stalin had agreed to divide Europe with his Western allies. In Western Europe, which he agreed should be an American and British 'sphere of influence', the Communist Parties were instructed to support the governments set up by the Allies. The Italian Communists joined a coalition with ex-fascists. The French Communists disarmed their partisans and joined the government of General de Gaulle. Only in Greece, where ferocious persecution from the Western-backed government forced the Communists to take up arms, and in Yugoslavia, where Tito's partisans were strong enough to ignore Stalin's orders, was the story any different.

The result was that the wave of radicalism came to nothing. In Eastern Europe, Stalin's tanks imposed state capitalism. In the West, the Communist Parties sat in coalition governments, until, with the outbreak of the cold war in 1947–48, they were kicked out of office, and forced into opposition, where most of them remain.

Since the war the Western Communist Parties have become much more independent of Moscow. The Kremlin is now a superpower with an enormous nuclear arsenal and can deal with Washington on equal terms without their help. They, for their part, have become conventional reformist parties committed to the parliamentary road to socialism.

Their strategy is still that of the popular front, although nowadays it is usually called the 'broad democratic alliance'. In the 1970s the Italian Communist Party advocated a 'historic compromise' with the main capitalist party, the Christian Democrats, while the Spanish Communist Party proclaimed its support for the monarchy and the armed forces. By the late 1970s and early 1980s even the mass Communist Parties of Italy, France and Spain were suffering from dwindling support.

The British Communist Party, always much smaller, has declined even more severely. During and after the Second World War it was able to build up considerable influence in the trade unions. Since the early 1960s that influence has been used in building 'Broad Left' alliances in the unions with members of the Labour Party. The approach was an electoral one — the idea was that the Broad Left should capture official union positions.

Its weakness was that it did not take into account the position of the trade union bureaucracy. It failed to recognise that even the most left-wing official will be likely, because of the very nature of his position, to seek compromises with the employers and hold back or undermine workers' struggles.

In recent years many Communist Party members have drawn the theoretical conclusion from this Broad Left strategy and joined the Labour Party. A majority of the survivors, around the monthly **Marxism Today,** have taken the notion of a popular front even further, rejecting class politics and espousing a 'broad democratic alliance' embracing Labour, Liberals, Social-Democrats, and even such 'progressive' Tories as Ted Heath and Francis Pym! Their opponents, who control the daily **Morning Star**, combine support for 'left' trade union leaders with nostalgia for the good old days of Stalin.

This steady drift to the right is contained within the very notion of a popular front, which the **Morning Star** faction still accept. For once you adopt a strategy of allying with classes whose interests are opposed to those of workers, 'progressive' or 'democratic' capitalists, for example, whose interest will always ultimately be profit, then you are bound to try to restrain workers' struggles.

By contrast, revolutionary socialism recognises first and foremost that the only class that will struggle for socialism, and has the potential to build socialism, is the working class.

WHERE WE GO FROM HERE

THE CLASS STRUGGLE IN BRITAIN

Many socialists have no faith in the ability of the working class to change society. The defeats of the past few years, the triumphs of Thatcherism, seem to have set workers' power at nought. Thus Labour's defeat in 1983 and Thatcher's victory over the miners were explained by some on the left with claims that the working class is disappearing.

Similar claims were made in the 1950s, when Labour lost three elections in a row. It's easy to forget what came in between. Between 1970 and 1974 the Tory government under Ted Heath launched a large-scale attack on the British trade-union movement. There ensued the biggest labour struggles for half a century. Indeed, the labour historian Royden Harrison has described the outcome of those years as 'the most extraordinary triumph of trade unionism in its long conflict with the government':

> The Labour Unrest of 1970–1974 was far more massive and incomparably more successful than its predecessor of 1910–1914. Millions of workers became involved in campaigns of civil disobedience arising out of resistance to the government's Industrial Relations Act and, to a lesser extent, its Housing Finance Act. Over 200 occupations of

factories, offices, workshops and shipyards occurred between 1972 and 1974 alone and many of them attained some or all of their objectives.

Strikes in the public service became more frequent and prolonged. Some of them began to exhibit an ominous concern with conditions of *distribution* as well as production. (Thus, some Health Service employees refused to supply privileges for private patients in public hospitals.)

But it was the coal miners, through their victories in the two Februaries of 1972 and 1974 who gave to this Labour Unrest a structure, a final roundedness and completeness which their contribution of 1912 had failed to supply to their earlier experience. First they blew the government 'off course'; then they landed it on the rocks. Finally, they compelled the Prime Minister to receive them in 10 Downing Street — which he had sworn he would never do — and forced him to concede more in 24 hours than had been conceded in the last 24 years. Then two years later their strike led him to introduce the three-day week . . . for which he was rewarded with defeat at the General Election.

Nothing like this had ever been heard of before!

How is it that an even more vicious Tory government under Margaret Thatcher did not meet the same sort of resistance? Let us look at the record.

During the long economic boom of the 1950s and 1960s strong shop stewards' organisation was built up in industries such as cars and engineering. The basis of this organisation was workers' economic power. Employers with full order books were prepared to buy off their workers with concessions on wages and conditions. Profits were high enough to permit a steady rise in real wages.

In the 1960s things began to change. British capitalism was under increasing pressure from foreign competitors. In response to this, with their share of world trade and profits falling, an offensive was launched by the employers and the state against shop-floor organisation. These attacks took a variety of forms — the Labour government of Harold Wilson imposed wage controls, while productivity deals were introduced by bosses in an attempt to remove the degree of control over production which some groups of workers had achieved during the boom.

The Heath government of 1970–74 merely took this process a stage further, introducing anti-union legislation whose main target was the shop stewards. Rank-and-file trade union organisation proved strong enough to beat off this attack, and indeed it spread to workers who had not previously elected shop stewards — civil servants and health workers, for example.

But shop stewards' organisation could not escape from the general limitations of trade unionism. It was, in the first place, sectional. During the boom, it had often been possible to win concessions from the bosses by downing tools within a particular section, without bringing the whole plant out. There was no tradition of shop stewards in different factories and industries linking together to form a wider organisation.

Secondly, shop stewards' organisation accepted the separation of economics and politics which is typical of trade unions. It sought to improve the situation of particular groups of workers within the framework of capitalism. Battles in the workplace had no political perspective. In the 1950s and 1960s they didn't need to. Workers could improve their position without taking on the state.

These limitations posed increasingly serious problems for shop stewards' organisation in the changed conditions of the 1970s. With employers and the state launching a general offensive against them, rank-and-file organisations had to develop a political strategy of their own.

Even with the victories over the Heath government in 1970–74, this didn't really happen. Shop stewards' political strategy, such as it was, amounted to: 'Kick out the Tories, vote Labour.'

After Heath had fallen in 1974, this left the workers' movement very vulnerable to a new and much more insidious attack. For the Labour government of 1974–79 sought to achieve by stealth what the Tories had been unable to win by frontal attack. Their chief weapon was the Social Contract, a deal struck between the Labour cabinet and the trade-union leaders which led to the imposition of drastic wage controls in the summer of 1975.

Although the social contract was signed at the top, between Wilson, Callaghan, and Healey for the Labour government, and Jones, Scanlon, and Murray for the trade unions, its spirit spread right through the movement. The idea of class collaboration — of government, bosses and unions working together — was accepted by shop stewards as well as full-time officials.

The result was that many shop-floor leaders were drawn into close co-operation with management. More and more senior stewards and convenors were now full-timers, and had become almost as alienated from their rank and file members as trade-union officials. Workers' participation schemes involved them constantly with management. Productivity deals took away in many workplaces the stewards' most fundamental role — that of bargaining over wages and conditions.

By the time Margaret Thatcher came to power in May 1979, rank-and-file organisation in key industries was much weaker than it had been five years earlier. Now the chickens came home to roost.

Two examples will illustrate this. One of the most dramatic 'successes' of workers' participation was at BL Longbridge, where the Communist Party convenor, Derek Robinson, worked very closely with management. He played a crucial role in heading off a rank-and-file rebellion against wage controls in 1977. But once he had served his purpose of weakening stewards' organisation, management could afford to take a much tougher line. Michael Edwardes, the new hard man appointed by Labour to head BL in 1978, and kept on enthusiastically by Thatcher, sacked Robinson. Thanks to the demoralisation of the workforce, and the cynical manoeuvres of the trade-union leaders, he succeeded.

An even more important case was that of the miners. It was they, after all, who had brought down Heath. But in 1977 the Coal Board, with the support of Energy Secretary Tony Benn, introduced a new bonus scheme. The aim was to divide the miners against each other, since under the scheme workers in highly productive pits would earn much more than their fellows elsewhere. Although rejected in a national ballot, it was imposed by the Miners' Union executive.

Furthermore the rank-and-file organisation which had provided the driving force of militancy in the coalfields in the late 1960s and early 1970s withered. Arthur Scargill had been a lay official and member of the Barnsley Strike Committee when he helped to organise the flying pickets of 1972. Little more than a year later he was elected Yorkshire area president of the NUM. Once he and his fellow members of the Broad Left in the Yorkshire coalfield had won control of the official machine, they ceased to organise unofficially, allowing the rank-and-file Barnsley Miners' Forum to collapse.

The effects were seen in 1984 and 1985. Right-wing officials in Nottinghamshire, which has many of the high-output, high-bonus pits, were able to organise mass scabbing and ultimately to form a breakaway union. Scargill, as national president of the NUM, fought for the militant tactics which had won in 1972 — above all, mass picketing. But his efforts and those of rank-and-file activists were sabotaged by area officials in the supposedly left-led Yorkshire, Scotland and South Wales coalfields. The folly of relying on a policy of electing left officials rather than organising the rank and file was dramatically shown in May 1984 when the 'left' Yorkshire area president, Jack Taylor, ordered his pickets to Nottinghamshire rather than sustain the mass blockade of Orgreave coking works.

So we are now paying the price of five years' Social Contract. Rank-and-file trade union organisation, weakened and demoralised by the class collaboration of the Wilson and Callaghan years, has not been able to face up to the offensive mounted by the tough, rabidly anti-working-class Thatcher government.

Workers' organisations have also been undermined by mass unemployment. During the boom years of the 1950s and 1960s, unemployment was negligible. This gave workers the confidence to take on the employers. The whip of mass unemployment is now being used consciously by the Tories and the bosses to discipline workers and clear militants out of the workplaces.

Economic crisis also raises the stakes. During the boom, going on strike didn't mean taking on the system. The 'national cake' was growing, and workers and profits could take a larger share of it. Now the cake isn't growing, and many sections of industry suffer acutely from falling profits. To fight now against the closure of an unprofitable factory, for example, means rejecting the whole profit system. Most workers, influenced as they are by the politics of class collaboration, are not yet willing to take this step.

Goodbye to the working class?

There will be those who still insist that the British labour movement has suffered more than a temporary defeat. Many despairing socialists argue that the decline of manufacturing industry in Britain means that the working class is vanishing. Others claim that Thatcher's rule amounts to 'creeping fascism'.

All this shows how important it is for us to keep our heads. Even though, in line with other advanced capitalist countries, the share of manufacturing industry in the workforce has declined, there are more than five million industrial workers in Britain today. There are millions of other manual workers — for example, those employed in the Health Service, who in 1982 fought a heroic six-month battle against the Tories.

There are also some ten million white-collar workers in Britain. The overwhelming majority are in the same basic position as manual workers. Many are women in low-paid and boring jobs such as clerical workers and shop assistants. They are as much part of the working class as miners and engineers. Indeed, recent years have seen a rapid growth in militancy and trade-union organisation among white-collar workers.

Nor have trade unions disappeared. Although the number of trade unionists has fallen, the main reason has been the rise in unemployment. There are still ten million trade unionists in Britain.

The Tories have only weakened, and not destroyed workers' organisation. A truly fascist regime would set out physically to smash the trade unions as Hitler and Mussolini did — seizing their assets and buildings, murdering thousands of leaders and activists, jailing tens of thousands.

Far from getting rid of the unions, Thatcher has depended in every victory she has won on the trade-union bureaucracy. The 1980 steel strike was lost, crucially, because of the failure of other unions, especially the Transport Workers' Union, to mount effective blacking. The 1982 Health Service dispute was doomed to defeat once the union leaders had refused to call an all-out strike. The TUC's sabotage ensured the miners' defeat.

And there have been victories. The water workers humiliated the government in their first all-out strike. The Fleet Street electricians closed down the national press for a day in solidarity with the health workers, and successfully defied the Tory Employment Act, showing that the spirit of 1972, of a fighting and united working class, is not dead.

The long-term downward trend in Labour's vote represents, not the disappearance of the working class, but the crisis of Labourism. Three periods of Labour government have left the structure of capitalism little altered. Again and again, Labour governments have cut public spending in areas that benefit workers, such as hospitals and schools, and attacked workers' living standards through wage controls.

It's little wonder that many workers feel little loyalty to the

Labour Party. Of course, Labour promises things will be different next time. But why should anyone believe them? Every government since the 1960s has left office with unemployment higher than when it was elected. Labour appeals to workers to rely on the state at a time when the state seems to have less and less power to manage the economy effectively.

The Tories have been able to exploit this disillusion. They have also been helped by the defeats of the past few years. With the level of industrial struggle so low, workers have few opportunities to acquire confidence in their own ability to change society. Thatcherism has fed off this mood of despair.

But the present downturn in the class struggle will not last for ever.

The experience of the international labour movement shows that there comes a point when some slight change in the situation — industrial recovery, or a political crisis — can spark off a great wave of strikes. The anger and humiliation built up in years of defeat boils over, and bursts into the face of the employers and the state. The most recent example of this was May 1968 in France.

The more intelligent representatives of the ruling class know that perfectly well. In the wake of the miners' strike large sections of big business decided that such a massive class confrontation was too costly in both financial and political terms to risk again. Thatcherism, they began to feel, had not delivered the goods: rather than achieving the massive cut in real wages needed to boost profits, the Tories had presided over a 5.5 per cent *rise* in real earnings in 1981–4. Perhaps, many in the City and industry began to speculate, another right-wing Labour government would be a more efficient instrument for cutting living standards, as it had been in the 1970s.

Socialists need to have at least as much foresight. We have to be realistic about the present situation, recognising just how bad things are, not giving way to fake optimism. At the same time, we have equally to resist phoney despair. The British working class is far from finished, and our job is to prepare for the upturn in the struggle when it comes.

There are those who argue that focussing in this way on the working class means ignoring problems other than those faced by people at work. What, they ask, about the oppression suffered by women — not just the lousy, low-paid jobs they get, but also the burden of housework they carry, the violence to which they are subjected at home and in the streets? What about the endless attacks that black people suffer — from racist immigration officers, police harassment and fascist hooligans?

Of course capitalism doesn't only exploit people at work. It oppresses us in many different ways — as women, as black people, as Jews, as gays. Capitalism isn't just a disaster as an economic system. It distorts and ruins people's lives sexually, culturally, psychologically.

The question is, though, what do we *do* about all this? It's very easy to pay lip service to what are sometimes called the 'autonomous movements' of blacks, women, and gays. This is what the Labour Party does, for example. But what do its policies amount to? At best they come to 'positive discrimination'. In other words a few token, well-educated, middle-class women and blacks will get top jobs. The mass of working-class women and blacks will get nothing.

The reason is a simple one. Racial and sexual oppression are so closely bound up with capitalism as to be inseparable from it. This means that the only way to get rid of racism and sexism is to get rid of capitalism. And the Labour Party isn't in business to do that, whatever politicians may say at the conference rostrum.

It all comes back to the question of *power*. Granted that we want to do away with racism, sexism, capitalism and what have you, who's actually going to do it?

The answer is, only the working class. The capitalist system rests on the exploitation of workers. By bringing workers together in large workplaces in order to exploit us, capitalism ultimately gives us the collective strength to paralyse, and overthrow it.

The tragedy of oppression is that it deprives people of power. Housewives are a fearfully oppressed group, isolated, condemned to drudgery, denied any positive role in society. But above all, they are powerless, a collection of isolated individuals without collective strength.

Black people at least are oppressed as a community. But even this gives them little power. The most a community can do is riot. And the state has long experience of dealing with riots. It may be taken aback by a sudden outburst, such as the inner-city riots of 1981 and 1985, but given time it learns its lessons, develops new tactics, buys off or isolates militants.

In the 1960s the United States was shaken by a wave of great ghetto risings — Harlem, Watts, Newark, Detroit, Washington. The slogan of 'Black Power' was raised by revolutionary groups such as the Black Panthers. In the 1970s the state remorselessly crushed the militants, murdering and imprisoning them. The 'moderates' were given a few concessions, and left with the invidious job of running America's decaying inner cities.

Where people have power is at work, in the collective organisations they build to fight the employers. That is where socialists have to concentrate their efforts. Does this mean ignoring women and blacks? Of course not — they are a crucial part of the working class. A higher proportion of black men work in manual industrial jobs than of white men. Women are over two-fifths of the workforce. It is at work that women and blacks too can develop the consciousness and confidence needed to sweep away their own oppression along with capitalism.

The Socialist Workers Party

Everything thus turns on the future struggles of the working class. If we are not to repeat the mistakes of the past, we must learn from those mistakes. If one had to sum up the reason why the British labour movement passed from the triumphs of the early 1970s to the abject condition of the 1980s in one word, it would be *Labourism*.

More than anything else, it was the commitment of shop-floor militants to the Labour Party and its parliamentary road to socialism which laid the basis for the weakening of rank-and-file organisation. Support for the Labour government, desire to keep it in office, caused workers' leaders — from the TUC General Council down to shop stewards in the smallest workplaces — to accept the argument that they should damp down their members' militancy and rely on Labour's Social Contract. The ideology of class collaboration penetrated every corner of the movement.

The danger is that this lesson will not be learned. Labour now stands for a 'partnership' involving employers, unions and government. This is just a code-word for wage-controls. It means that a future Labour government would repeat the disasters of the 1960s and the 1970s.

So when it comes to trying to rebuild rank-and-file organisation, this must be done on lines different from the past. We need workplace organisation whose horizons are not those of the section or the single workplace, but which reaches out to unite workers across the class. We need workplace organisation that understands and relies upon its own strength — for so long as it is tied to the Labour Party, the same old mistakes are likely to be repeated.

Merely rebuilding shop stewards' organisation can't solve these problems if it continues to operate within the limits of trade unionism. The only way in which workers can become politically independent of Labourism is through the development of a revolutionary socialist party.

Building such a party means going against what most socialists in Britain are doing. They are to be found in the Labour Party, trying to push it leftwards. This is a hopeless task. Every attempt to win Labour to genuine socialism has failed, with the left defeated or absorbed into the mainstream.

The future of socialism in Britain depends upon the creation of an independent revolutionary party. We in the Socialist Workers Party believe that we have made a start at building such a party.

The origins of the SWP lie in the revolutionary socialist tradition. For a generation, from the 1930s to the 1960s, the working-class movement was dominated by Stalinism and social democracy. Socialism was identified with the power of the state, with socialism from above, imposed on people by parliament or party. The authentic Marxist understanding of socialism as the self-emancipation of the working class was preserved only by a handful of revolutionaries on the very margins of the working-class movement.

These revolutionaries drew their inspiration from Leon Trotsky, with Lenin the leader of the Bolshevik revolution. For opposing Stalin's dictatorship, Trotsky was removed from all his posts and eventually expelled from Russia in 1929. For the rest of his life he struggled to keep alive the flame of the October revolution, until he was murdered by an agent of Stalin in 1940.

Trotsky's fundamental idea was that revolution could succeed only if it spread internationally. Confined to one country, it would succumb to the forces of international capitalism. This analysis has been amply confirmed by the fate of the Russian state, and of other 'socialist' countries.

Nevertheless, the years of the economic boom that followed 1945 were bad ones for revolutionaries, during which it was hard for us to get a hearing. Trotsky had predicted that the Second World War, like the First, would be followed by a wave of revolutions. He underestimated the hold of Stalinism and social democracy on the mass of workers after twenty years of defeat. When these revolutions did not happen, Trotsky's followers splintered into a myriad of tiny squabbling sects.

One of these was the Socialist Review group, formed in Britain in 1951. Its members were distinguished by their rejection of Trotsky's view that Russia was a 'degenerated workers' state'. They argued that it was, rather, a state capitalist society. They also soon recognised that Western capitalism had been able temporarily to stabilise itself, thanks to massive arms spending, and predicted that the boom would give way to a new period of crises.

For most of the 1950s the Socialist Review group had only a handful of members. Renamed the International Socialists (IS) in 1960, it began to grow very gradually, until by 1968 it had some four hundred members. IS doubled in size that year, as students involved in college occupations and in opposition to the Vietnam war joined the group.

The election of the Heath government in 1970 led to dramatic confrontations between workers and the state, and by the time of Heath's fall in March 1974 the International Socialists had 4,000 members, and our paper, *Socialist Worker*, was selling 30,000 copies a week. The change of name to the Socialist Workers Party came in 1977. For the first time since the degeneration of the Communist Party in the late 1920s, revolutionary socialist ideas had a working-class audience in Britain.

The years since 1974 have been far more difficult. But our voice is still strong, and as we have shown, a voice for revolutionary socialism is more necessary then ever. The question is how to make that voice more widely heard. We seek to do so by holding regular political meetings, selling our weekly paper, *Socialist Worker*, and working around whatever workers' struggle there is.

Our aim in all these activities is the same, to widen the audience for revolutionary politics. In every battle that takes place, we do not merely strive for victory. We seek to encourage workers to learn the lessons of the struggle, and to place it in the wider context of the confrontation between capital and labour. By so doing, we hope that more will come to understand that there can be no final victory without the overthrow of the capitalist state.

Building a revolutionary party in Britain today, capable of providing a socialist alternative to Labour, is essential. All the signs are that the Kinnock-Hattersley leadership, should they gain office, will preside over a Labour government even more disastrously right-wing than its predecessors of the 1960s and 1970s. One possible consequence of such a social-democratic regime is dramatically illustrated by France under Mitterrand — disillusioned workers sidetracked into racism, embracing the fascism of Le Pen.

There is only one sure guarantee against such an outcome in Britain — the largest possible socialist alternative to Labour. Thousands of people were inspired and radicalised by the miners' strike. Most of them naturally gravitated towards the left of the Labour Party. They find themselves faced with a strident right-wing leadership and a relentless purge of socialists. The space which the Militant Tendency especially enjoyed to organise openly as socialists within the Labour Party is disappearing. The choice is increasingly between knuckling under, which means moving rightwards and accepting Kinnock's leadership, or standing firm, which means breaking with Labourism and organising an independent socialist party.

We in the Socialist Workers Party hope that as many socialists as possible choose the latter option. At the end of the miners' strike and then again in autumn 1985 we appealed to the Militant and other left-wing activists to join us in a new united socialist organisation outside the Labour Party, an organisation within which we and others could freely organise for our politics. Such an organisation would provide a powerful pole of attraction for the thousands radicalised by the miners' strike, who will otherwise succumb to Kinnock.

Unfortunately, our proposal seems to have been spurned by the Militant leadership. In these circumstances we will press ahead with our own smaller alternative, the Socialist Workers Party. We have no illusions of grandeur, but we can create a network of socialist activists who are prepared to listen to us, and to follow our lead in struggle.

Such a network will be of decisive importance in the future. For, as we have already seen, the anger and frustrations built up over the years of defeat will at some time fuse with renewed confidence to cause an explosive upturn in the class struggle. The presence within the labour movement of a revolutionary party with a periphery of militant socialists would mean then that revolutionary socialists could actually *influence* the outcome of the struggle and give socialist ideas and socialist action a chance.

A socialist revolution has four elements — a mass strike, workers' councils, an insurrection to overthrow the existing state, and a revolutionary party. Even in the difficult circumstances of today we can prepare for each of these aspects of the upturn.

The key to the mass strike is the workplace. Here socialist activity must be rooted. There are no short-cuts to be made by capturing ward Labour Parties or trade-union executives.

Workers' councils emerge only when the entire class in on the move. But we can begin even now to prepare for workers' councils. Such councils unite the working class as a whole, breaking down the divisons between men and women, black and white, skilled and unskilled. We can start the work of overcoming these divisions by continually arguing for, and striving to achieve solidarity between these different sections of workers.

An insurrection depends on the active and willing support of a majority of workers. But the key to its success lies in the relationship between socialists and their fellow-workers. Even in the smallest strike we can learn how to draw the less militant workers in struggle, to open their minds to revolutionary ideas, to advance and retreat as the situation dictates.

Finally, we have the time to create the precondition of any revolutionary party — a body of activists who both understand the basic ideas of revolutionary socialism and share considerable experience of the labour movement.

The two great revolutions at the end of the First World War, in Russia 1917 and Germany 1918, illustrate the importance of this. The Bolsheviks in Russia had been trained by fourteen years of victory and defeat. The revolutionary left in Germany broke with the 'old house' of social democracy only in December 1918, after the revolution had begun.

The Bolsheviks multiplied rapidly in numbers and influence. Those who had been on the edge of the party before the revolution now joined, and brought with them others who were now thrust into politics for the first time. At the same time, the party had a stable core of experienced revolutionaries.

The German Communist Party in the crucial months of 1918–19 lacked such a core, and did not have deep enough roots in the labour movement to draw many workers into its ranks.

The existence of a revolutionary party made the difference

between victory and defeat at the end of the First World War. In the long run, whether we work to build a revolutionary party *now* in Britain could make that sort of difference for socialism tomorrow.

There should be no mistake — the stakes are very high. It isn't just that the world economy stumbles from brief boom to long slump without any sign of a genuine recovery. The shadow of nuclear war hangs over the planet. Each time before that world capitalism has found itself at an impasse, its tensions have been resolved through world war. The same tensions are all around us. Two vast power blocs confront one another, each with enormous nuclear arsenals, profound economic difficulties, and restless subjects. If the conflicts of world capitalism again turn to war, this time the outcome will be total destruction.

During the First World War, Rosa Luxemburg said that the choice lay between socialism and barbarism. We now know the face of barbarism well, after the death camps of Auschwitz and the nuclear holocaust of Hiroshima. Only the world working class, by tearing the wealth and weapons from our rulers' hands, can save humanity from the prospect of crisis ended only by annihilation.

With socialism, we can go on to use the world's resources, and human beings' accumulated knowledge and skill to change the face of the world, to create a world in which poverty, exploitation, and war are only bad memories.

It is with that goal in mind that we in the Socialist Workers Party set out. We have no illusions about the scale of the task, or about the limitations imposed by our size, influence, and talents. We don't regard ourselves as the elect, the bearers of the truth. We know that only the working class can transform society. We don't seek to put ourselves in place of that class. We seek only to make workers conscious of their interests and their power, and to direct that power at the capitalist state.

We appeal to all who agree with us, to join us in building a revolutionary socialist party. We ask those who will only go part of the way, to work with us. Together we have a world to win ■

JOIN THE SOCIALIST WORKERS PARTY

Socialism, the emancipation of the working class, is the act of the working class. That is why the Socialist Workers Party is a party of activists, seeking always for the point at which our effort will carry us one step further on the road to socialism.

We appeal to all who agree with us to join us. If you can only go with us part of the way, then work with us for our common goal. Return the form below to: The National Secretary, Socialist Workers Party, PO Box 82, London E3. ★

I would like to join the SWP. Please put me in touch with my local branch. Please send me more information about SWP meetings and activities. (delete as applicable)

NAME _____

ADDRESS _____

_____

★ For a list of revolutionary socialist organisations in other countries, see the early pages of this book.

READ SOCIALIST WORKER

the weekly newspaper of the **Socialist Workers Party**, with up-to-date news and political analysis of workers' struggle throughout the world. 25p every week from SWP members and left bookshops.

■ For a special introductory subscription, send £2.50 for the next 10 issues (postage included) to: **Socialist Worker** Circulation Department, PO Box 82, London E3.

Other publications from the Socialist Workers Party

HOW MARXISM WORKS
by Chris Harman
A basic introduction to the ideas of Marxism, and how they guide action for
socialism today.
£1.50 plus 20p postage

THE GREAT STRIKE
by Alex Callinicos and Mike Simons
The miners' strike of 1984–5 was a struggle of epic proportions, in which the Tory
government under Margaret Thatcher mobilised all the forces of the state to crush
the miners' union, including paramilitary police attacks of a ferocity unseen for 50
years or more. This is a story of courage and determination.
£3.95 plus 60p postage

WOMEN AND THE STRUGGLE FOR SOCIALISM
by Norah Carlin
Feminists want to change the world, to make women free and equal. Socialists, too,
want to change the world, to get rid of the rotten society of which women's
oppression is part, and build a better one based on workers' power. But are the two
struggles the same, or must they be separate — as many feminists proclaim?
95p plus 25p postage

WHAT IS THE REAL MARXIST TRADITION?
by John Molyneux
'All I know,' said Marx, 'is that I am not a Marxist.' What in the 1870s was a neat
dialectical joke has since been transformed into a major political problem. The
hundred years since Marx's death have seen the emergence of innumerable and
conflicting 'Marxisms'. This book sets out to untangle the knot.
£1.95 plus 40p postage

RUSSIA: THE MAKING OF THE REVOLUTION
by Steve Wright
Between the revolution of 1905, which was brutally suppressed, and that of 1917,
which brought to power the world's first workers' government, lie the most crucial
twelve years in the history of the socialist movement. This pamphlet examines the
building of the Bolshevik Party, the instrument that brought the world closer to the
achievement than ever before, or since.
75p plus 20p postage

All available from good left bookshops, or by post from
BOOKMARKS
265 Seven Sisters Road, London N4 2DE.